To Raef and Nadiya

Contents

Introduction

Friedrich Nietzsche was a German philosopher. He lived from 1844 to 1900 and is most famous for his declaration that 'God is dead' and his consequent belief that we must therefore create a new man, a 'Superman'. Nietzsche is probably the most widely read philosopher in the modern world, yet he also continues to be the most misunderstood. His writings were almost totally ignored during his lifetime, and up until the mid-twentieth century his philosophy was neglected and badly translated. Up until then his influence has been claimed in areas as diverse as vegetarianism, anarchism, Nazism and religious cultism. It is only more recently that Nietzsche has undergone something of a rehabilitation and a deserved recognition has emerged that here was a man who ranks amongst the great and original thinkers of the modern age.

Nietzsche was the first philosopher to fully confront the prevailing loss of religious belief in Western Europe with his declaration that 'God is dead'. What Nietzsche meant by this was that society no longer had a need for God, for He had outlived his usefulness. Nietzsche was therefore calling for humanity to stand on its own two feet without the support of faith or dogma of any kind. Nietzsche, therefore, was not only attacking religious faith, but also a belief in objective values or truths. We must *choose our own values*. The reason people persisted in a belief in God or truth, Nietzsche argued, was because of their reluctance to face the reality of the situation; it is a form of self-deception. Rather it is better to face and, indeed, to embrace, the temporary nature of existence and the apparent meaninglessness of life.

Nietzsche suffered from severe illnesses throughout much of his life, including severe migraines which meant he often lay in a darkened room, unable to leave his bed. He went insane in January 1889, and his illness and insanity may well have been the result of contracting syphilis, although he suffered from headaches even as a boy. Nietzsche, however, saw illness in a positive way, providing him with the inspiration to write and think: great works come from suffering, he believed. Indeed, he was able to write his greatest works during perhaps the times of his worst suffering, both physically and mentally. Works such as *Thus Spoke Zarathustra*, *Beyond Good and Evil*, and *The Genealogy of Morals* were all written between 1883 and 1887.

Nietzsche was born at a time of great change. The age of the telegraph had arrived in the year of Nietzsche's birth, Karl Marx's *Communist Manifesto* was published when Nietzsche was four and, in the same year, revolutions were breaking out across Europe with the growth in new values and ideas such as popular liberalism, nationalism and socialism. Over the next two decades, Germany (under Bismarck) and Italy achieved political unification, Austria and Prussia eliminated feudalism and, in 1861, Russia freed the serfs. From the 1870s the second phase of the Industrial Revolution led to mass production of goods and the mechanization of society. Importantly, from a religious perspective, belief in God was on the decline: Marx had declared it to be the opium of the masses and Charles Darwin's (1809–82) theory of evolution raised serious religious questions regarding the authority of the Bible. Nietzsche was to present a critical eye over these changes: of the dangers of Enlightenment ideals, of increasing mechanization and secularization, of democracy and liberalism and of nihilism. In many respects, Nietzsche can be seen as a prophet of his time, yet also out of step with his time, as prophets often are. Whilst many head like lemmings towards the cliff edge, singing the praises of science and political enlightenment, Nietzsche stands on the top of a high mountain and looks down from another perspective, one of caution and warning of the possible dangers of this new age.

He is certainly the most controversial and notorious philosopher to have lived, as well as being one of the world's most interesting and scintillating you will come across, in the realms of philosophy at least. When people think of Nietzsche today they associate him with his harsh criticisms of religion, specifically Christianity, as well as his attack on the belief in 'another world'. Previous to his rehabilitation, however, many did not regard him as much of a philosopher at all but, even worse, someone who should be banned from the bookshelves. The reasons for this perception of

Nietzsche will be unravelled as you read on, and even the current understanding of him can be considered as open to debate. The fact that today you can attend Nietzsche conferences, where he is discussed amongst serious and highly professional philosophers, should be sufficient evidence that here we are talking about Nietzsche as a very serious philosopher indeed.

Nietzsche's texts – Abbreviations

Ecce Homo: **EH**
Thus Spoke Zarathustra: **TSZ**
The Birth of Tragedy: **BT**
Beyond Good and Evil: **BGE**
The Twilight of the Idols: **TI**
The Antichrist: **AC**
The Gay Science: **GS**
The Genealogy of Morals: **GM**
Untimely Meditations: **UM**
Human, All Too Human: **HAH**

Nietzsche's early life 1844–79

Nietzsche was born on 15 October 1844 in Germany. Although his father died when Nietzsche was only five years old, his childhood was, on the whole, a happy one. He was doted upon by his female relatives. As a child, Nietzsche was very religious, but as a young teenager he began to question religious tenets. At university, he ceased being a Christian altogether and abandoned his studies in theology. In his twenties, he became increasingly ill, the likely cause being syphilis. This ill health was to plague him for the rest of his life. Nietzsche published his first major work, *The Birth of Tragedy*, in 1871. It was not, however, well received in the academic world and he resigned his university post due to illness in 1879.

Nietzsche's background

The importance of a person's childhood on their views in maturity should never be underestimated. Nietzsche himself states clearly in his writings that our philosophies are moulded by our upbringing, which is why he is so critical of attempts by philosophers to be objective and to believe they can ever step outside themselves.

Nietzsche was born on 15 October 1844 in Röcken, a municipality in the district of Burgenlandkreis in Saxony-Anhalt in Germany. Even today Röcken is a small village with a population of less than 200. You can still see the house, the Pastor's house, where Nietzsche was born, and which has now become a museum. You can also visit the ancient church (one of the oldest in Saxony) where he was baptized, his village school, and the well-kept family grave where he is buried next to his sister Elisabeth and his parents. Röcken was surrounded by farms, and the nearest town, Lützen, was a half-hour's walk away and was itself a very small market town.

Nietzsche's ancestry has been traced back to the sixteenth century of some 200 German forebears. None were aristocrats and most were small tradesmen such as butchers and carpenters. However, he is also the heir of some 20 clergymen. Nietzsche's grandfather was a superintendent (the equivalent of a bishop) in the Lutheran Church, and the philosopher's father, Karl Ludwig, became pastor for the village. Friedrich's mother, Franziska Oehler, was the daughter of the Lutheran pastor of a neighbouring village. The first five-and-a-half years of Nietzsche's life were spent in a parsonage, and even after that he was brought up in a pious environment. It is curious to note that the philosopher who came to symbolize more than any other the rejection of religious dogma, was brought up within such an observant household. His philosophy has, as a result, been seen as a deliberate rebellion against a strict, oppressive and conformist upbringing. Yet the Lutheran Church resembles more the Anglican rather than some fundamentalist, puritan church. In fact, the Lutheran tradition has contributed greatly to German intellectual and cultural life and has encouraged cultural and social improvement. There is every indication that the young Friedrich had a happy and fulfilling childhood, and he never spoke in his writings of any kind of rebellion against his upbringing. If anything, the young Nietzsche was more strict and conformist than his peers.

Nietzsche's father was 30 years old when, in 1843, he married the 17-year-old Franziska. Nietzsche shared a birthday with the reigning King of Prussia and so was named Friedrich Wilhelm after him. After Friedrich, they gave birth to a daughter, Elisabeth, in 1846, and a second son, Joseph, in 1848. Also residing in the house were Nietzsche's two rather dotty aunts and Franziska's widowed mother. By all accounts, Nietzsche's mother possessed a great deal of common sense and unquestioning piety, but had not been well educated. The first years of Nietzsche's life were quiet ones as the family settled down to their existence together. The descriptions of the house and its surroundings conjure up an idyllic setting, with a small farmyard, an orchard, a flower garden and ponds surrounded by willow trees. Here Nietzsche could fish and play, exercising his imagination as all children do. According to his sister Elisabeth's memoirs, Nietzsche took up talking rather late to the extent that, at the age of two-and-a-half, his parents consulted a physician who suggested that the reason he hadn't spoken was because the family were so excessive in their devotion towards him he did not feel the need to ask for anything. His first word, apparently, was 'Granma', an indication of the female influence in the household, and by the age of four he began to read and write.

Tragedy strikes

Although childhood was, on the whole, a happy one for Friedrich, in 1849 tragedy struck with the death of his father. Karl Ludwig was only 36. A year later, Nietzsche's younger brother also died. The traditional family existence was shattered and they were compelled to leave Röcken to go to the nearby walled town of Naumburg. The young Friedrich now lived with his mother, sister, two maiden aunts and a maternal grandmother. Women, therefore, surrounded Nietzsche, and his younger sister, especially, doted upon him. Nietzsche's mother was still very young, but she was never to remarry.

In many respects, life at Naumburg would have differed little from Röcken, for it too was a small town that saw or cared little for the outside world. Nietzsche was to live there until he was 14. His mother, as a result of legacies left by her own mother on her death in 1856, had the financial means to set up a home of her own.

Nietzsche attended the local boys' school where he made his earliest friends, Wilhelm Pinder and Gustav Krug. Pinder, at the age of 14, wrote an autobiography in which he makes regular mention of Nietzsche, describing his initial encounter with the young Friedrich as one of the most important events in his life. The picture Wilhelm presents of the boy Nietzsche is of someone who loved solitude and had a pious, tender temperament whilst having a lively, inventive and independent mind. Significantly his character is portrayed as someone who displayed the virtues of humility and gratitude and was preparing himself for a future vocation as a pastor. Pinder's father was a town councillor and lover of literature, and he used to read Goethe to the three boys. Krug's father was an amateur musician, and we can detect Nietzsche's life-long love of music originating here as he took it upon himself to learn to play the piano.

Nietzsche's education

In 1851, the three boyhood friends were transferred from the town school to the private preparatory school until 1854. Here, Nietzsche received his first taste of Latin and Greek. They all went on to the higher school, the *Domgymnasium*, until 1858 when Nietzsche – no doubt due to his intellectual talents – was awarded a free boarding place at the exclusive and strict Pforta school. Nietzsche was studious, certainly, but he enjoyed outdoor activities such as walking, swimming and skating, and grew to be physically well-built. However, he suffered from illness throughout most of his life and it was during these years that the headaches began, possibly linked also to his short-sightedness and the large amount of reading and writing he did as a child.

Pforta School was disciplined and traditional. Pupils were awoken at 4 a.m., classes started at 6 a.m. and continued until 4 p.m. There were further classes in the evening. The school concentrated on a classical education – especially Latin and Greek – rather than mathematics and the sciences. Nietzsche developed an enthusiasm for poetry, literature and music, as well as scholarly criticism, which first led him to doubt the tenets of the Bible.

When he went to the University of Bonn in 1864 to read philology (the study of language and literature) and theology he had already ceased to believe in the existence of God. At the university, Nietzsche soon abandoned the study of theology altogether, a subject which he had probably only agreed to do because of his mother's eagerness for him to become a pastor. Nietzsche never really settled down in Bonn and decided to go to Leipzig University in 1865 where he became much more studious.

During the Leipzig years (1865–9) there were a series of life-changing encounters. First of all, it was during this period that Nietzsche quite likely contracted syphilis after attending a brothel. Syphilis was incurable and could result in a life of periodic illness leading to insanity and early death. Secondly, while wandering around a second-hand bookshop, Nietzsche came across *The World as Will and Idea* (1819) by the German philosopher Arthur Schopenhauer (1788–1860). Nietzsche became a 'Schopenhauerian'. Schopenhauer's pessimistic view that the world is supported by an all-pervasive will that pays no attention to the concerns of humanity fitted well with Nietzsche's feelings at the time. He also read the *History of Materialism* (1867) by the philosopher and social scientist F.A. Lange (1828–75) which introduced Nietzsche to a form of Darwinism. And thirdly, on 28 October 1868, Nietzsche announced his conversion to the hugely influential composer and musical theorist Richard Wagner (1813–83) after hearing a performance of the *Tristan* and *Meistersinger* preludes. Only 11 days later he met Wagner in person. During that brief meeting, in which Wagner turned on the charm and entertained on the piano, Nietzsche discovered Wagner was also a Schopenhauerian. Wagner was born the same year as Nietzsche's father and bore some resemblance to him, and so developed into a father figure for Nietzsche.

Nietzsche's university professor considered him to be the finest student he had seen in 40 years. Consequently, Nietzsche was awarded his doctorate without examination and was recommended for a chair in classical philology at Basel University in 1869. At the age of 24, Nietzsche was already a university professor.

The professor

Between the ages of 6 and 34 – a total of 28 years – Nietzsche was never to leave the environs of the classroom for more than a few months during the holiday periods. This was, therefore, a period of intense and cloistered learning and it is perhaps no wonder that Nietzsche was to reject a career in academia. For the next ten years at Basel University, Nietzsche became less interested in philology and more enthusiastic towards philosophy. For Nietzsche, however, philosophy was not to be found by being immersed in books – which, essentially, was all that philology was concerned with – and he longed to expand his horizons. However, the lure of a salary and being able to support his mother was an important inducement in keeping the post.

Basel was essentially a German town, although it rested within Switzerland. In taking the post, the university asked that he become a Swiss national so that he would not be called up for Prussian military service at any time that would interfere with his work. Nietzsche ceased to be a citizen of Prussia, but never succeeded in satisfying the residential requirements for Swiss citizenship. From 1869 onwards, Nietzsche remained stateless. Nonetheless, this did not prevent him from applying to be a nursing orderly for the Prussian forces during the Franco-Prussian War. It is quite possible that Nietzsche saw this as his opportunity to escape from the world of books, at least for a while. However, he suffered from diphtheria and ended up being nursed rather than being the nurse. After which, he returned to his teaching.

Despite his reservations, Nietzsche proved to be an able and popular teacher. Students spoke of his enthusiasm and their sense that this man had been transported through time from Ancient Greece; such was his knowledge and explication of the subject. A famous incident in class was when he suggested that the students read the account of Achilles' shield in Homer's *Iliad* over the summer vacation. At the beginning of the next term, Nietzsche asked a student to describe Achilles' shield to him. The embarrassed student had not read it, however, and there followed ten minutes of silence during which Nietzsche paced up and down and appeared to be listening attentively. After the time had elapsed, Nietzsche thanked the student for the description and moved on!

Nietzsche also developed his own physical appearance. By most accounts he was a smart dresser, almost to the extent of being something of a dandy. He began to cultivate his celebrated moustache that, in a famous photo of 1882, covered the whole of his mouth. There is another photo of Nietzsche with his mother taken in 1890, which shows the moustache reaching down to his chin!

From 1871, Nietzsche started to become seriously ill: an illness that was to dog the rest of his life. While he had suffered from headaches since he was a child, now they were mostly in the form of severe migraines; so relentless that he could not eat and would have to remain in bed in a darkened room for days on end. These recurrent illnesses always left him exhausted, and so it is all the more amazing that he was able to work so prolifically. During an absence from university due to illness he worked on his first book, *The Birth of Tragedy* (1871). Although loved by Wagnerians, as it sang the praises of the composer, it was attacked by academics as little more than Wagnerian propaganda and lacking in scholarly study.

Nietzsche's illnesses became steadily worse, forcing him to spend less time at the university. He was also becoming disillusioned with Wagner, who he began to see as a sham philosopher. Also, Wagner had moved to Bayreuth, which put an end to the weekend visits. In 1878, Nietzsche wrote *Human, All Too Human*, a quite definitely anti-Wagnerian work which caused Wagner to say that Nietzsche would one day thank him for not reading it. This work, though stylistically a great improvement on *The Birth of Tragedy*, was still viewed as lacking in intellectual rigour or coherency. This, together with increased bouts of severe illness and a loss of interest by students in his teaching, caused him to resign his university post on a small pension in 1879.

The influence of Wagner

Nietzsche's dissatisfaction with the academic world is reflected in his work. Although he did write some scholarly articles in the 1860s, he was a reluctant adherent to the accepted norms of the academic style. Nietzsche always considered himself as something of a poet and a composer. He liked to improvise on the piano and wrote music himself. As a pupil at Pforta, Nietzsche formed a literary and musical society with some friends called 'Germania'. The friends would meet regularly to read aloud the works they had written or composed. Certainly, he saw his writing as an outlet for his artistic capabilities and indeed much (though not all) of his philosophy is extremely poetic and dramatic. Nonetheless, in his early work especially, this can come across as evidence of an immaturity and a deflection from any kind of rigorous scholarly coherency that would have been expected of a university professor. Coupled with this, his relationship and blind love for Wagner infected his early writing. Nietzsche does not really begin to find his own voice until his split from the composer.

Wagner was always a controversial and larger-than-life figure. Although he had already written four operas, it was *Tannhauser* in 1845 that caused the most controversy. Because of its innovations in structure and technique it both confused and shocked his audiences. He was also a political radical, taking an active part in the revolution in Germany in 1848, which required him to live in exile in Zurich where he started composing the famous *Ring* trilogy. The political ban against Wagner was lifted in 1861 and he returned to Prussia. Despite marrying an actress in 1836, Wagner had a number of affairs, most notably with the daughter of the composer Liszt, Cosima von Bulow. They married in 1870.

Wagner was more than a composer, however. He was also a musical theorist, and his thought on political issues such as nationalism and social idealism greatly influenced the nineteenth century. His music was strongly nationalist, and he had also expressed clear anti-Semitism in his writings, making him an attractive composer for the Nazis. Despite this reputation, Wagner did affect a revolution in the theory and practice of operatic composition and it was this factor that would have appealed to Nietzsche and his early belief that music acted as a salvation.

In retrospect it seems surprising that someone as perceptive as Nietzsche seemed to be so taken in by the flamboyant ego of Wagner. It is said that, during Nietzsche's weekend visits to Tribschen, Wagner would behave as if in one of his own operas. Dressed extravagantly, with only his own music playing, he would waft across the gardens and corridors of his luxurious villa amongst busts of himself, talking mostly about himself! However, this picture is most likely an exaggeration, and Nietzsche did learn much from being in the company of Wagner, for he recognized the composer's ego as a need to dominate others, to exert his power over them. Undoubtedly, Wagner was a charismatic figure, and it is quite impressive what he could persuade others to do for him. From studying Wagner, Nietzsche developed his own views on psychology and on the desire for man to dominate others. In this respect, Wagner's eccentricities were a minor irritation. However, during the early Leipzig years, Nietzsche's infatuation with Wagner and his willingness to sacrifice his own career if need be to serve under the composer came across only too obviously in his early writings, especially with his first major work, *The Birth of Tragedy*.

2

Nietzsche's later life and death 1879–1900

Nietzsche's severe, debilitating headaches grew worse and he had to give up his academic career in 1879. He then spent the next ten years wandering in various countries for the sake of his health. These years proved to be very productive years in terms of his writing: by 1885, Nietzsche had completed *Thus Spoke Zarathustra*, followed by *Beyond Good and Evil* the next year. The year 1888 was, however, the last of Nietzsche's sane life, although it was also the year when he started to receive recognition. Nietzsche spent his final years (1889–1900) completely mad. He was cared for by his sister, Elisabeth Nietzsche, an anti-Semite and pro-Nazi, who edited Nietzsche's works and presented him, falsely, as the Nazi philosopher. Nietzsche died on 25 August 1900 and was given a Christian burial, against his own wishes.

Nietzsche's 'wanderings'

Throughout much of his mature life, Nietzsche was godless, stateless, homeless and wifeless. For the next ten years (1879–89) Nietzsche, with only the clothes on his back and a trunk full of possessions, wandered through Italy, southern France and Switzerland. He had been advised by the doctor to seek more clement environments for his health, and this he attempted to do. Despite the illness, Nietzsche now started to produce his greatest, most mature works. These include *Dawn* (1880), which attacks the idea that morality has any objective basis, *The Gay Science* (1882), which first declares the death of God, and *Thus Spoke Zarathustra* (1885), which talks of the 'Superman'. Perhaps Nietzsche's finest work of all, *Beyond Good and Evil* (1886), brings together all of Nietzsche's philosophy in the most systematic way he ever gets, yet Nietzsche remained largely unknown and unread.

Nietzsche's 'wanderings' should not be seen as periods of isolation and solitude, of leading a hermit existence in the same way as Zarathustra's ten-year retreat to the mountains. Nietzsche continued to have close friends and even, perhaps, a lover for a very brief time, during his ten-year spell. He could quite probably have ended a life of relative solitude if he had so wished, but the fact is he did not wish it and probably required periods of solitude as this suited his nature. There were times of melancholy and regret, of wishing for a loving wife and children, but this always seemed to pass as he embraced his philosophical enterprise with such passion.

Nietzsche spent the winter of 1880–81 in Genoa finishing his work *Dawn*, declaring that, 'This is the book with which people are likely to associate my name.' And '... I have produced one of the boldest and most sublime and most thought-provoking books ever born out of the human brain and heart.'

Lou von Salomé (1861–1937) and Paul Rée (1849–1901)

One of Nietzsche's close friends was Paul Rée (1849–1901). Nietzsche first met Rée in 1873 when the latter, as a non-student, chose to attend a series of lectures given by Nietzsche on The Pre-Platonic Philosophers. Rée was five years younger than Nietzsche and, by all accounts, much more precocious. Rée was the son of a Jewish landowner and was also an atheist, but his view of existence as having no ultimate meaning led Rée into pessimism, whereas it tended to liberate Nietzsche.

Originally, Rée had been a law student but became attracted to philosophy, and he was also interested in the importance of psychology as a way in to understanding the beliefs of human beings. More specifically, Rée was interested in the religious and moral beliefs of humans, explaining religious experience as an attempt to interpret the world, rather than as witness to an objective reality. Nietzsche was particularly influenced, however, by what Rée had to say about morality.

Back in 1876, Nietzsche had taken a year's leave of absence from his university teaching to stay at a villa in Sorrento, Italy. He was joined here by Paul Rée and a 21-year-old Basel law student named Albert Brenner. Nietzsche saw the villa as a 'monastery for free spirits' and later wrote, 'In Sorrento I shook off nine years of moss.' The three 'free spirits' worked on their books and they read (usually Rée would read aloud to Nietzsche) the works of the French moralists such as Montaigne, La Rochefoucauld and Vauvenargues. Inspired by Rée and the French, Nietzsche wrote aphorisms which were brought together and published as *Human, All Too Human* (1886) and *Daybreak* (1881). Rée, for his part, wrote *The Origin of the Moral Sensations*; a theme which has resonance in much of Nietzsche's own writing from this time on. The visit to Sorrento was undoubtedly a turning point for Nietzsche as it reinforced his decision to give up his professorial post and become a 'free spirit'.

In 1882, Rée, while staying in Rome (Nietzsche was in Sicily at the time) met and immediately fell in love with the 20-year-old Lou Salomé. Salomé was born in St Petersburg, the daughter of a Russian general of Huguenot descent. She left Russia in 1880 with her mother to study at the University of Zurich, but suffered from a severe lung disease that compelled her to look to better climates to recover. Her doctors, who gave her only a few years to live, suggested she head south and hence she ended up in Rome. No doubt her feeling that she would not live long gave her an extra passion for life, and an enthusiasm for the study of philosophy that would have attracted many to her. It certainly had an effect on Rée as they would walk the streets of Rome night after night discussing their ideas. Rée was so excited about Salomé that he would write to Nietzsche about her. Nietzsche himself soon became smitten with Salomé. When Nietzsche, having spent three weeks in Sicily, turned up in Rome in April 1882 it was only a matter of days before he proposed to Salomé. Rée had also proposed to Salomé but her response to both of them was that she was not interested in marriage, but would rather form a kind of intellectual *ménage à trois* in which the three of them would share an apartment in Vienna or Paris, writing, studying and debating. This idea certainly seemed to appeal to Nietzsche, who often dreamed of a 'secular monastery'.

Such a threesome was bound to fail eventually, given the egos and competitive nature of the three characters. But the *ménage à trois* did not occur immediately, rather Salomé spent some time with Rée and his mother in West Prussia before, in August, spending three weeks in Tautenburg with Nietzsche and his sister Elisabeth. Nietzsche's sister took a dislike to Salomé and considered the idea of such a threesome insane. At Tautenburg, Salomé and Nietzsche were housed in separate apartments and they would take long walks together. Plans were drawn to set up the *ménage à trois* in Paris. Nietzsche made inquiries amongst his friends in Paris regarding accommodation, but what he had not realized was that Rée had become increasingly jealous of Nietzsche in the relationship. Realizing that Nietzsche presented a possible threat to his own romantic intentions towards Salomé, Rée arranged for himself and Salomé to live far away from Nietzsche in Berlin. Nietzsche was never to see either of them again.

The final years

From 1882 Nietzsche's thoughts were already on _Zarathustra_, with Part One written by February 1883.

Reading the opening pages of _Zarathustra_ we can see this as autobiographical, as it paints a picture of the suffering that Nietzsche himself now felt as a result of the Salomé affair.

The year 1888 was the last of Nietzsche's sane life, although it was also the start of his fame... He spent the beginning of that fateful year in Nice, stayed in Turin from April until June, spent the summer in Sils-Maria, and then returned to Turin in September. It was, in this respect, a year of his usual wanderings. But, in other respects, it was very different. In his correspondence, Nietzsche reported that his health was improving and he felt a sense of joy and elation with life, not recognizing that these feelings of euphoria were symptomatic of forthcoming megalomania.

Added to this tragedy of oncoming madness was the fact that Nietzsche was never to appreciate the success and influence his work was to have, for undoubtedly Nietzsche courted notoriety and wanted success. It was on the very first day of 1888 that the first ever review of Nietzsche's whole work appeared in a German newspaper. A few months later, in April, the internationally renowned Danish critic and biographer Georg Brandes (1842–1927) gave a series of popular lectures on Nietzsche at Copenhagen University. Nietzsche had finally arrived, yet his letters were becoming more and more bizarre, evidence of the looming insanity.

In this final year of sanity, Nietzsche was as prolific a writer as ever. He wrote six short books: _The Wagner Case_; _The Twilight of the Idols_; _The Antichrist_; _Ecce Homo_; _Nietzsche contra Wagner_; and _Dithyrambs of Dionysus_. So are these works in any way a reflection of Nietzsche's approaching insanity? In these works he does not introduce any new philosophy and nor does he contradict what he has previously said. There is evident continuation from his previous work and the structure is generally tight and presented in a magnificent poetic style. These works deserve attention, therefore, and show no evidence of Nietzsche having lost his intellectual capacity. Quite the contrary, in fact.

On 3 January 1889, according to a well-known although possibly apocryphal account, Nietzsche walked out of his lodgings and saw in the piazza a cabman beating his horse. Nietzsche cried out, ran across the square and threw his arms around the neck of the horse. At that moment he lost consciousness. A crowd gathered and the landlord of Nietzsche's lodgings carried the still unconscious Nietzsche back to his room. When he finally came to, he shouted, sang and punched away at the piano. When he calmed down he wrote a series of epistles to his friends and the courts of Europe declaring that he, signed 'the Crucified', would be going to Rome in five days' time and that all the princes of Europe and the Pope should assemble.

Elisabeth Förster-Nietzsche (1846–1935)

Much of Nietzsche's legacy is closely related to his sister's less favourable legacy. Elisabeth Nietzsche, more than any other person, is responsible for the misunderstandings that have accompanied Nietzsche's philosophy to this day. When Nietzsche started writing poetry at the age of eight, it was the six-year-old Elisabeth who collated them for him. At such an early age she already felt responsible for the work and life of the shy Friedrich.

When Nietzsche collapsed in madness he left behind mounds of unpublished material at his various lodgings. Elisabeth established an Archive in a house in Naumburg that would become a museum of Nietzsche's works. As well as his works, however, Nietzsche himself was lodged in a room as one of the exhibits. Incapable of coherent speech, he was exhibited to important visitors and dressed in a white robe like a Brahman priest. Elisabeth turned her brother into a prophet, surrounding him in mystique and turning his madness into something seemingly superhuman.

In 1896 Elisabeth moved the growing Archive to Weimar, considered the cultural centre of Germany. In fact, during World War II, Weimar was the centre for cultural propaganda, with Nietzsche as the official philosopher of Nazism. When the Russians occupied Weimar after the war, the Archive was sealed and remained so until the fall of the Berlin Wall in 1989.

The collected works of Nietzsche brought Elisabeth fame and fortune and she became the official mouthpiece for her brother. However, in collecting his works, she would ignore any of his philosophy that she did not agree with, forge letters that she claimed Nietzsche had written to her that praised her, and wrote a popular biography of Nietzsche that was full of lies. The greatest sin of all was that she collected Nietzsche's unpublished notes into a book called *The Will to Power*. She claimed that this was Nietzsche's final testament, his true philosophy, whereas it is full of discarded thoughts and poorly written notes that Nietzsche had no intention of publishing. Although of historical interest, it is a shame that it is still quoted as an authority of Nietzsche's philosophy.

Nietzsche, at a time before his mental collapse and the fallout with his sister, had once written to Elisabeth requesting that, at his death – for he always believed he would die young – he should be given a pagan burial, with no priest at his grave. However, when he died on 25 August 1900, Elisabeth gave him a full Lutheran funeral and buried him in a coffin with a silver cross.

The Birth of Tragedy

When Nietzsche published *The Birth of Tragedy* it was heavily criticized by scholars for being too ambitious and, to a large extent, naive. Even in his early writings, Nietzsche demonstrated a literary style that was poetic, but not 'academic' according to the standards of the time. From *The Birth of Tragedy* until his last writings, Nietzsche was always critical of the modern man of science and progress – his 'theoretical man'. He is critical of Socrates, and therefore Plato, because of their over-emphasis on the importance of reason, and their belief in objective values. In *The Birth of Tragedy*, he emphasizes the importance of art and, more generally, culture as an affirmation of life. This is in contrast to the scientific, 'deconstructive' picture of the world presented by modern man. Nietzsche pictures the world as essentially cruel, but vibrant. If, therefore, we are to find any 'truth' at all, we must share in this view of the world.

Despite Nietzsche's acknowledged brilliance and precociousness, this first work did not help to cement that reputation in academic circles; in fact it did more harm than good. Its publication was heavily criticized by scholars.

Nietzsche's dissatisfaction with the academic world is reflected in his work as he either refused or was unable to write within the accepted norms of the academic style.

The 'theoretical man'

The Birth of Tragedy deserves a chapter of its own because the work itself stands out as a unique and interesting thesis. A first impression may make one wonder why Nietzsche chose to consider Greek tragedy given his intention to produce a work that would have contemporary cultural significance, but this ignores the importance of Greek culture at the time of Nietzsche. It was not, then, as it may be seen by many today (quite wrongly), a 'dead' subject with little importance except for those who had the luxury to study it. Whilst, on the one hand, there was a push towards industrialization and marketplace values, there was, on the other hand, an increase in disillusionment with the goals and values of modernity accompanied by a looking-back to bygone eras, most notably that of Ancient Greece. It was felt by many, poets and artists chief amongst them, that the Greeks possessed a set of values, a spirituality and an affirmation of life that seemed to be desperately lacking amongst industrialized, scientific, modern man.

The 'theoretical man', the man of science and progress, is what Nietzsche consistently condemns until the end of his writing career, and it certainly possesses modern-day concerns where success is measured by how much money and property you possess rather than by, for want of a better word, 'wisdom'.

Interestingly, Nietzsche presents Socrates as an example of this 'theoretical man'. In the philosophical realm, Socrates is considered one of the greatest philosophers, yet Nietzsche frequently criticizes him as the 'archetype' of those modern, alienating values. Therefore, when Nietzsche talks of the philosophy of Socrates he is not usually making any distinction with that of the philosophy of Plato. There were certain aspects of the philosophy of Socrates and Plato that Nietzsche was particularly in disagreement with.

Firstly, the Platonic view that there is such a thing as objective truth. This was a response to the belief in **relativism**: that the morals and beliefs are a product of a particular time and place and, therefore, there is no such thing as 'right' and 'wrong'. Secondly, Plato argued that the world we live in is essentially an illusion, a poor image of a better, perfect world. The role of the philosopher, therefore, was to seek out this better world rather than be preoccupied with everyday existence. Thirdly, Plato believed that the true world can be accessed through the power of reason. Mankind has both instinct and the capacity to reason, but frequently prefers to follow instinct and ignore reason like that of other animals. Plato argues that, by exercising reason – the intellect – mankind can know what truth is. Finally, Nietzsche lays the blame of over 2,000 years of this kind of philosophy and the death of tragedy at the foot of Socrates. In particular the whole philosophical concern with **metaphysics**, the speculation on what exists beyond the physical world, Nietzsche considered to be an error and a distraction from what really mattered.

For Socrates, tragedy was no longer required because reason could remove the fear of death. Although Nietzsche admired the genius of Socrates, as well as his achievements, he saw Socrates as representative of the desire to *explain*, to engage in argument and counter-argument, rather than accept that ultimately there are no explanations. Also, Nietzsche was not against reason and science; he would be the first to praise its achievements and its role in the enhancement of life. What he condemned was the regard of reason as providing *answers*, delivering mankind from a state of ignorance.

Apollo and Dionysus

In *The Birth of Tragedy*, Nietzsche gave a lot of importance to Art as a medium through which we comprehend the world. He took on board this dualism of Art and Nature under the principles of Apollo and Dionysus. These two Greek gods are presented as a metaphor for two fundamental principles:

* **The Apollonian:** Nietzsche compares the Apollonian with dreams. In a dream you express fantasies but these are a way of forgetting the world rather than confronting the realities of the world. Apollonian art is exemplified by painting and sculpture. In the same way that we conjure up images in dreams, we do the same in painting. But these paintings are only representations of the world; they are fantasies that allow us to turn our backs, at least for a while, from the world we live in. Apollo, then, is an artistic style: that of form and clarity, and so is also represented in sculpture and architecture most commonly.

* **The Dionysian:** Nietzsche compares Dionysian art with intoxication. Nietzsche did not necessarily mean alcoholic intoxication, but rather the kind of ecstasy that can also be caused by means other than alcohol, for example, through sexual intercourse, dancing or religious activities. Like the Apollonian, the Dionysian is a mechanism for fleeing from reality, but intoxication is not the same as fantasy. Dream fantasies are an individual and private experience when you turn away from the world. Dionysian intoxication, however, is not about forgetting the world, but forgetting your *self* and experiencing more of a mystical communal union. Dionysian art is more akin to music and poetry. Nietzsche accepted that the distinction between painting and music was not always so clear. It is quite possible, for example, to have Dionysian painting, and Nietzsche was aware that music had Apollo as its patron god. The more important distinction is how one *responds* to the work of

art, rather than the work of art itself. Nietzsche sees Apollo as expressing individuality, whereas the Dionysian revels in music and dance and so breaks down the individual like some kind of Sufi *dhikr*.

The importance of culture

The importance of culture is another theme that remains throughout all of Nietzsche's works. When Nietzsche was at Basel in 1869 he met, and became acquainted with, the historian Jakob Burckhardt ('friend' would be too strong a word in this case, as Burckhardt for his part kept his distance), whose most famous work, *The Culture of the Renaissance in Italy*, was published in 1860. Burckhardt, also something of a pessimistic Schopenhauerian, was particularly interested in the history of culture, as opposed to military or political history, and he argued for three major forces of existence: state, religion and culture. For Nietzsche, culture (which in his case could well include religion) was the highest objective, more so than, say, economics or science.

If, Nietzsche argued, the Greeks were supposed to be as happy and sunny as pictured, then there would be no need for Apollonian art, yet there is plenty of evidence of Greek tragedy to show that the Greeks suffered immensely. In Greek tragedy we are presented with the images of gods and men, of heroes and monsters, as a way of transforming their fears for such things, in the same way dreams are projections of our own fears and doubts. The Dionysian element is the tragic chorus present in the tragedy. The chorus would narrate the story through song. They acted as an artistic substitute for the Dionysian rites by allowing the audience to identify themselves with these singing, dancing characters and therefore participate within the tragedy themselves and not be mere spectators. This was therapeutic, allowing audiences to feel a sense of unity with their fellows, with the chorus, and with the drama of the tragedy as well as to feel god-like themselves.

Life is tragic, and in *The Birth of Tragedy* Nietzsche wrote a phrase that has often been quoted since: 'Existence and the world are eternally justified solely as an aesthetic phenomenon' (*BT*, 5). A *moral* point of view may well argue for democracy and the welfare state, for the greatest happiness for the greatest number, but an *aesthetic* point of view – which Nietzsche advocates – is not concerned with such 'levelling'. If we are looking for recurrent themes in Nietzsche, then undoubtedly a key theme is his criticism of modernity, of the way we are now. This criticism rests upon two key features of modernity. First, we have lost what he calls our 'metaphysical solace' when faced with the certainty of death. Second, we have killed myth. Nietzsche says that the modern man is a myth-less man; when, for example, we go to the theatre we can no longer experience the 'miracle' which, for children, is a matter of course (*BT, 23*). We have lost the magic – in particular of art – because we have become too critical when studying history. The modern man breaks things down (is 'deconstructive'), reduces everything, rather than sees things in a more holistic manner.

The value of Greek tragedy

Nietzsche portrayed Greek tragedy as an interactive, mystical and unifying experience that provided a therapeutic outlet for a people who were sensitive to the suffering and uncertainties of everyday life, and in which mankind is in tune with Nature. Man is no longer an artist but a work of art. Art possesses form and so by making life a work of art it gives the world a form, a structure. Nietzsche quotes the greatest tragedians as being Sophocles and Aeschylus in the fifth century BC.

Although the Ancient Greeks suffered, Classical Greek tragedy, Nietzsche believed, presents a balanced picture of the world. Whilst understanding that individuals inevitably suffer in this life, there is solace in being aware of the underlying energies that pervade the world. As mentioned, Nietzsche saw Socrates as the precursor of an alternate, disabling, vision of 'optimism': an over-rationalized, logical, scientific view of the world that represses the emotions, the human instincts. At this time, and remember Nietzsche was only 28, he saw *The Birth of Tragedy* as a manifesto for change, as a call for a revolution. While such rhetoric is rarely the place for an academic text, it was heartfelt, hence Nietzsche's frustrations with what he increasingly saw as dusty academia.

4

the revaluation of all values

In *The Gay Science*, published in 1882, Nietzsche introduces the character of a 'madman' who enters a busy market place and asks, 'Where is God?' The madman is mocked by the people in the market, which causes him to say, 'We have killed him, you and I.' What Nietzsche means when the madman says we have killed God is not that God is literally dead, but that our belief or need for God is dead. Whilst Nietzsche's morality is notoriously difficult to interpret, what we can say with certainty was that he was opposed to the belief in objective moral truths. Ultimately, Nietzsche was not so much concerned with providing a table of values. What mattered was that values should be life-affirming. His attack is against what he calls the 'herd' morality, with its characteristic feature of '*ressentiment*', by which Nietzsche means the expression of a feeling of inferiority and powerlessness.

Morality

Nietzsche's morality permeates all of his works, but the most systematic works of moral philosophy are *Beyond Good and Evil* and its 'sequel' *The Genealogy of Morals*.

Nietzsche is not so much concerned with the fact that our beliefs are false, but rather with the belief *about* these beliefs. That is, why should we hold the beliefs that we do? At the beginning of Nietzsche's epitome *Beyond Good and Evil*, he raises the question of why we want truth; why not *untruth*? It is frequently the career of philosophers to seek for truth, and Nietzsche targets them for his main criticism. He believed the most important question should not be what is true or not but the extent to which a belief supports life and maintains a species. When philosophers make claims to truth they are merely presenting a preconceived dogma that tells you more about the philosopher's beliefs than anything to do with truths. For Nietzsche, this is especially true in the case of moral philosophy; an attempt to make a science of morals, to establish an objective morality.

In *The Gay Science*, Nietzsche first declares that God is dead: 'God is dead. God remains dead. And we have killed him' (*GS*, 125). By this, Nietzsche means that society no longer has a use for God; the belief does not in any way help the survival of the species, rather it hinders it. The implications of this are important for ethics, for with the death of God comes the death of religious, especially Christian, morality: a morality that has underpinned Western culture since the fourth century.

Slave morality

Two years after *The Genealogy of Morals*, Nietzsche wrote *Ecce Homo*, and states clearly the intention of the First Essay of *Genealogy*:

> **The truth of the first inquiry is the birth of Christianity out of the spirit of ressentiment, not, as people may believe, out**

of the 'spirit' – a countermovement by its very nature, the great rebellion against the dominion of noble values.

(*EH*, III)

In fact, Essay 1 is an elaboration of the relatively lengthy Section 260 of *Beyond Good and Evil*. The very title of the book with the use of the word 'genealogy' is important as it is provocative of the time to so much as suggest that morals *have* a genealogy – that is, a history and development – rather than adopting the view that morals are just 'there' waiting to be discovered. This, then, is Nietzsche's main argument of the whole text, but as stated in Essay 1: morals are not universal and immutable, but are historical products that are therefore contingent creations of particular people at particular times with particular *motives*. The emphasis on motives is important here, because where Nietzsche is particularly original is in getting us to question the value of our morals rather than to assume that moral values are intrinsically valuable. This enterprise is also indicated in the title *Beyond Good and Evil*: to understand what we mean when we use moral terms such as 'good' and 'evil' we need to go *beyond* them. In addition, Nietzsche thinks moral philosophers are wrong in believing that modern man is morally better than past generations and he especially attacks utilitarianism, which was the dominant moral theory at the time. The fact that Nietzsche claims that our morality has a traceable, evolved ancestry at all would have shocked many a reader in his time, for morals were seen as given by the divine lawgiver God and so there is no genealogy to trace. If the lawgiver disappears, then so does the law and the fear that what will result will be moral anarchy. Yet Nietzsche argues that morality can be explained in naturalistic terms, without the need for a God or gods. They are natural phenomena that have evolved as a result of the need to keep societies together and to check instinctual drives that would destroy the unity of the group if they were allowed free reign. Therefore, morality is a result of circumstance, and it is the circumstance that comes first which is then followed by morality, not the other way around.

For Nietzsche, morality:
* is a result of circumstance, not the other way round
* serves a useful function in that it binds the fabric of the group
* can, however, outlive its use and become a hindering custom.

If morality ceases to serve a useful function, yet continues to be maintained by society, then this might stunt the growth of that society because we continue to live by rules that are no longer applicable to the world we live in. Nietzsche looked to his own society and saw it to be in a state of decay for this very reason, i.e. that it looks to the old values; the old *Christian* values. When Nietzsche talks of the morality of Western Europe as being the product of a particular time and people, what he had in mind in terms of the people were Christian slaves and at the time and place of the Roman Empire *circa* the first to the third centuries AD. This is why he refers to morality of his time as 'slave morality' as opposed to the 'noble morality' possessed by the Romans before the coming of Christianity. What is needed is a *new morality*. By considering the genealogy of morals, Nietzsche hoped to demonstrate why we have the values we do. This way, if we still continue to hold such values, we are at least aware that they are effectively redundant.

In considering why Christianity originates with the slaves of the Roman Empire, Nietzsche argued that they saw this as a way of release from bondage. As the slaves were not powerful enough to literally free themselves from their masters, they were consoled by religious belief that provided them with spiritual liberation. Christianity, like everything else, is an expression of the will to power. The first Christians were slaves under the Roman Empire and so the only way they could assert any kind of superiority over the Romans was to assume a higher spiritual status. This was achieved, according to Nietzsche, by inverting the values of society. For example, values such as compassion or pity were regarded by Christians as righteous values that would lead to reward from God, whereas other values such as self-interest were seen as sinful.

Ressentiment

The real motive for promoting such values was not because there actually is a God that enforces such values, but because the slaves resented the status of the Romans and wanted to possess their power. This is what Nietzsche means by the French term **ressentiment**. The slave feels relatively impotent compared with the master and he is not able to accept the idea that he is treated worse than others. This leads to hostility, to resentment, yet he is unable to release this hostility because of his enslavement. What is the slave to do? He cannot simply use brute force, as this will result in him being in a worse state than before, and so he must use *guile*.

In order to enact revenge upon his master, the slave uses the weapon of moral conduct. It consists of getting the master to acquiesce to the moral code of the slave and, as a result, appraise himself according to the slave's perspective. As Christians, of course, the slaves should not have the option of revenge, for they should 'turn the other cheek'. However, so successful were the slaves in their guile and secrecy that they managed to disguise their revenge under the cloak of pure intentions.

As the master estimates his own worth according to the values of the slave, he will perceive himself and his actions as evil and reprehensible. His old aristocratic values will be discarded, as he feels morally obliged to do 'good' in the Christian sense. Nietzsche portrays the Roman aristocrat as physically powerful, healthy and aggressive. These qualities remain but, unable to express them internally, they are directed inwards. The aristocrat ends up punishing himself rather than others.

For Nietzsche, slave morality could only have arisen out of hatred and fear. The slave's morality is a reaction to the actions of others. That is, when someone does something to you that you resent, then you class it as 'bad' and, consequently, you create a morality in opposition to this: that is 'good'. If you are frightened of your neighbour you react by wanting your neighbour to love you and this is why love is a Christian virtue. The master's morality, however, is not a reaction to others at all. The master has no need to view himself according to the actions of others, but rather affirms himself. He does not require to be loved or for everyone to conform. The master can also hate, but this hatred is discharged in a 'healthy' manner through direct action, rather than, in the case of the weak, through resentment.

Nietzsche is presenting both an historical and psychological portrayal, and it is dubious on both counts. From the psychological point of view, Nietzsche portrays the slave as someone with so much pent-up aggression that it becomes poisonous unless it is expressed in some natural way. This resembles the equally unconvincing psychological theory that children should be allowed to let out their aggression, otherwise it will remain bottled up inside and express itself in later life in some other form. From the historical perspective we must allow Nietzsche a certain degree of artistic licence so long as the point is made. He is specifically thinking of Christianity when he talks of religion. Nietzsche was not talking about all religions, for he admired the Greek religion. His main concern with Christianity was its dehumanization: because God is regarded so highly, as perfect and all-good in fact, then it logically follows that man regards himself so lowly, as necessarily imperfect and sinful. Nietzsche did also criticize Jewish slave morality for being the originator of Christian morality.

One of the misunderstandings of Nietzsche's philosophy needs to be made clear at this point. Nietzsche was not an anti-Semite. It is clear from his correspondence that he hated anti-Semites and, in fact, all racist theories. This misunderstanding derives from reading Nietzsche out of context, always a dangerous thing to do, as well as Nietzsche's youthful enthusiasm for Wagner's ideas, and Wagner most definitely was an anti-Semite. Nietzsche's sister Elisabeth, who married an anti-Semite, interpreted her brother's works as anti-Jewish. Nietzsche's language can be easily misinterpreted, especially when he uses such phrases as 'blond beast' (*GM*, 11) when referring to the masters. This has been used as an indication that Nietzsche supported German nationalism and Hitler's views on Aryanism. However, what Nietzsche actually meant by 'blond beast' was a reference to the lion as king of the beasts.

Nonetheless, Nietzsche's views on the master-slave morality are perhaps his most controversial and it is easy to understand why this is the case when a few of the main points are considered:

* The master morality made a distinction between 'good' and 'bad'. 'Good' applies to those who are united, noble and strong. 'Bad' refers to the slaves who are weak and base.

* This notion of 'good' and 'bad' therefore is *not* moral. 'Bad' merely meant to be one of the herd, the 'low-minded'. 'Good' meant the noble and intellectual.

* Christianity reinterpreted 'good' and 'bad' as 'good' and 'evil'. 'Good' was now represented by the life and teaching of Jesus Christ; such values as altruism. 'Evil' became what for the masters was previously 'good'.

Nietzsche obviously admires the masters, and there is a certain pro-aristocracy element to him here. Nietzsche evidently approves of a firmly defined class structure and had a disdain for the moral and social mores of the masses.

The priests

Nietzsche specifically attacks the Christian (and, before them, the Jewish) priests in their role of promoting the slave morality. The priests were in the unique position in society in that they were both strong and weak at the same time. They were weak in relation to the aristocratic masters, but they were strong spiritually because they were God's agents on earth. The pastoral, as opposed to the royal, power that the priests possessed was used as a tool for social control and promoting the moral ideal of the herd.

Although he refers to the herd, or slave, morality as promoting the teachings of Christ, Nietzsche places the blame firmly on St Paul as the one who misinterpreted Jesus' teachings. In fact, Nietzsche regards Jesus as a member of the master morality because Jesus was a life affirmer who criticized the Jewish priests for using religion as a means of social control. St Paul, who travelled across the Roman Empire establishing churches in the first century, set the stage for the development of the slave morality and corrupted Jesus' teachings to suit his own ends. The ethic that was endorsed was one of asceticism and self-denial. St Paul was a Roman citizen and was educated in Greek philosophy, and so he made Christianity acceptable to the Romans by incorporating Greek philosophical ideas, especially the Platonic view of dualism. An outlook was presented based on a dualistic worldview: this world being one of necessary suffering, but preparation for a better world in the next life. This world was inferior, therefore, to the next world, and the priests had turned Christianity into life denying, instead of Christ's life affirmation.

The revaluation of all values

For Nietzsche, the declaration that 'God is dead' sets man free to become his or her own being, to be the 'Superman'. Their morality is a rejection of the herd morality. These are the elite; people who have mastered their own will to power and created life-affirming values to live by. The most crucial value for Nietzsche was that we should be life-affirming. The Superman, therefore, is one who realizes the potential of being a human being and is not consoled by a belief in the next life. The Superman has mastered himself and creates his own values.

The practical implications of his philosophy are not something Nietzsche gave much consideration to. Nietzsche is not a democratic philosopher, for he is not a supporter of the values of the common herd. He believed in the great man, the hero, the Superman, who should be a law unto himself. However, it is difficult to see how a society that consisted of such an elite, that establishes its own values, would function in society. They would, presumably, look towards the masses with contempt, and one wonders how the Superman could live either amongst the masses or even amongst themselves. There would be inevitable conflict, although Nietzsche would have welcomed this provided it led to a revaluation of values.

Nietzsche's rejection of such Christian values as turning the other cheek, loving your neighbour, and compassion for those that are suffering, might come across as somewhat callous. For one reason or another, many are unable to stand on their own two feet or face the realities of life, and so there is a need for compassion. However, Nietzsche did not despise such values as compassion; rather it is the use of it as a psychological prop instead of looking towards one's own resources. Nietzsche's own almost crippling illness plagued him for most of his life, but the last thing he would have wanted was compassion or pity.

Nihilism

One of the stated aims of *Beyond Good and Evil* was to liberate Nietzsche's Europe from what he considered to be a decline into decadence, nationalism and stupidity. His concerns for the future of Europe turned out to be prophetic, of course, and this helps to understand why Nietzsche himself was often taken to be something of a prophet after his death; an image his sister Elisabeth was more than happy to promote. The title *Beyond Good and Evil* can be misleading, as it suggests that we must cast aside all values, that there are no values and, consequently, the coming of the Superman heralds a breed that can do as it pleases, without any regard or concern for others. This, however, is not what Nietzsche meant to express.

Nietzsche's philosophy, in a desire to give it some kind of label, has sometimes been described as **nihilism**. Coming from the Latin *nihil*, meaning 'nothing', the term suggests negativity and emptiness, of a rejection of all values and a belief in nothing. Yet Nietzsche could be a very positive, joyful and affirmative philosopher. We can categorize two types of nihilism; neither of which Nietzsche falls into but was nonetheless influenced by:

* Oriental nihilism
* European nihilism.

1 Oriental nihilism

Schopenhauer was heavily influenced by what he understood of Buddhist teachings and, when he talks of extinguishing the self and that the world we live in has no ultimate reality, it is this form of nihilism that he is considering. It possesses the following characteristics:

* Because the world we live in is not real our attachment to it is an illusion.
* Life is without sense or point, merely an endless cycle of birth and rebirth.
* To find salvation we must escape from this world and extinguish the concept of the self.

2 European nihilism

The Russian author Ivan Turgenev (1818–83) was the first to introduce the nihilist to the novel. In his greatest novel, *Fathers and Sons* (1862), the hero is Bazarov, an idealistic young radical dedicated to universal freedom but destined for tragedy. This novel reflected a nihilism that existed in the latter decades of nineteenth-century Europe:

* Nihilists consisted mostly of the younger generation who rejected the beliefs and values of the older generation.
* Rejecting the beliefs of their elders such as religion, tradition and culture, these nihilists claimed to believe in 'nothing'.
* However, the nihilists replaced traditional beliefs with a belief in science. Instead of seeking salvation in the next life, the nihilists looked to a better understanding of this world as the future hope.

3 The 'nihilism' of Nietzsche

In both Oriental nihilism and European nihilism, there still exists a belief in salvation; that there can be a form of order and values. Nietzsche, however, goes much further than this:

* All beliefs systems, whether it is science, religion, art, or morality, are fictions. They are merely instances of the will to power.
* This world is the only world, even if it is valueless. There is no 'unity', no 'truth'.
* This fact should not lead to pessimism, to a 'will to nothingness'. Rather, we should adopt a Dionysian 'yes' to life.

To say the world is 'valueless' is not to say that it has little worth. Rather, it does not make sense to say one thing has more 'value' than another, because there is no such thing as a scale of values. Nothing has value; there are no facts, no 'better' or 'worse'. This was a rejection of the beliefs of so many philosophies and religions that there is an objective world. These religions and other metaphysical propositions often endorse a **Correspondence Theory of Truth**. This theory holds that when we use terms like 'God', or 'good' or 'bad' or 'justice' we are making reference to an actual 'God', an actual 'justice' and so on; that is, these terms *correspond* to a reality. For Nietzsche, there is no reality for these terms to correspond to.

Amor fati

Amor fati: to love your fate! For European nihilism, especially of the Russian variety, a rejection of traditional values had political implications with the call for a revolution. For Nietzsche, his main concern was with the psychological impact of the acceptance that there are no truths. It could well lead to pessimism and despair or the attitude that 'anything goes'. For Nietzsche, he saw nihilism as a positive affirmation of life, to be freed of the burden of hope in an afterlife, in salvation. You should love your fate without the need of fictions and false securities to comfort you.

Nietzsche's 'nihilism' finds its culmination in the doctrine of the eternal recurrence. Man must not only accept his fate and, indeed love his fate, but also to embrace this purposeless existence as recurring again and again for infinity. The person who can do this deserves the title 'Superman':

* The Superman rejects the belief that there are objective values or values of any kind.
* The Superman does not, as a result, become a pessimist or suffer from despair; rather he embraces life and loves his fate (*amor fati*).
* Even when faced with the prospect that he will have to live exactly the same life again, the Superman's *amor fati* is not dented. Even existence in its most fearful form is a joyful one.

5

the will to power

The concept of the will to power is one of Nietzsche's most famous contributions to the philosophical tradition, and yet it is a notoriously difficult concept to interpret. The main reason for this difficulty is that Nietzsche is never particularly explicit in his account of the doctrine. Many previous scholars have looked to his unpublished notes for enlightenment, and in these notes Nietzsche seems to present a doctrine of the will to power as a metaphysical explanation for the nature of everything. Yet this interpretation is not only unoriginal, it goes against Nietzsche's published criticisms of presenting any kind of metaphysical doctrine. Perhaps the best understanding of the will to power is more a subjective interpretation of the world, given Nietzsche's view that all beliefs are essentially subjective. It may be the best interpretation our empirical observations can currently provide.

What is the will to power?

The debate over what the will to power actually is and how much importance should be attached to it centres on two differing interpretations:

1 **An objective explanation for everything**. Nietzsche wants to give us a metaphysical picture of the world – a 'theory of everything' which explains the world of experience but, nonetheless, is 'beyond' the physical (hence 'metaphysical').

2 **A subjective interpretation**. This is not asserting that there is a world 'out there' beyond the physical, but is simply putting forward the will to power as a subjective interpretation.

The will to power is certainly one of the most famous contributions that Nietzsche made to philosophy, yet it is also a concept that is subject to a variety of differing interpretations by scholars. Nietzsche, for his part, is not always helpful in his own articulation of the will to power either, which inevitably opens him up to speculation and disagreement amongst his readers. Much writing on the will to power, especially early scholarship, places this concept at the heart of Nietzsche's philosophy, as the underlying concept for all of his philosophical views on such things as morality, art and nature. More recent scholarship, however, has raised questions as to whether Nietzsche really gives us a strong doctrine of the will to power *at all*.

Has the importance of the will to power for Nietzsche's philosophy been over-played? It is certainly curious that Nietzsche seemed to drop any reference to the will to power in his last major work, *Ecce Homo*. This omission is significant because in this work Nietzsche reflects upon his ideas in all his previous works. To make no mention of the will to power at all certainly suggests that he no longer considered it important. In addition, in 1886, Nietzsche wrote a series of new prefaces to *The Birth of Tragedy*, *Human, All Too Human*, *Dawn* and *The Gay Science* in which he reflected upon his major philosophical themes, yet the will to power was again not mentioned.

However, although he may have decided against developing the will to power in his published works, this is not to say that it was not a doctrine that ceased to preoccupy him – quite the opposite, in fact. The reason Nietzsche wrote new prefaces for many of his earlier books was because he was in the process of changing publishers as he had learnt that his old publisher had two-thirds of his books stuffed in a warehouse with little attempt to push sales. After writing books for 15 years, it would have been a huge disappointment to Nietzsche to discover that his publisher had made little effort to sell his books. By launching with a new publisher, Nietzsche hoped for a fresh beginning, and so wrote a series of new prefaces. He also decided to start a new work with the title *The Will to Power: Attempt at a New Interpretation of Everything that Happens*. The title alone is quite revealing and does suggest that Nietzsche believed in at least the *possibility* of the will to power as an important contribution to his philosophical enterprise. This project became almost an obsession (and certainly a therapeutic aid against depression) for Nietzsche and, for that reason if for no other, it should not be surprising that his sister and Peter Gast should collect his notes together into a work with the title *The Will to Power*. Nietzsche's project was intended to be a major four-volume work that would have a coherent structure unlike his previous collections of aphorisms and short essays. However, in the autumn of 1888, he completed *The Antichrist* which was intended to be the first volume of his great work, yet ended up being the whole work itself. Nietzsche had previously given up on the title *The Will to Power* anyway, and was leaning towards 'Revaluation of All Values' which, in retrospect, seems more fitting to his lifelong enterprise. Hence he wrote, 'My revaluation of all values, which has *The Antichrist* as its main title, is finished.'

It is, then, perhaps going too far to say that Nietzsche places no importance on the will to power. The terms 'will to power' and 'power' are used explicitly throughout many of his works, as well as implicitly. The fact also that Nietzsche was so preoccupied with it through much of his sane life suggests it has some value, even if Nietzsche saw it more as a tentative experiment rather than a fully worked-out doctrine.

Quote from *The Will to Power*:

> **And do you know what 'the world' is to me? Shall I show it to you in my mirror? This world: a monster of energy, without beginning, without end; a firm, iron magnitude of force that does not grow bigger or smaller, that does not expend itself but only transforms itself; as a whole of unalterable size, a household without expenses or losses, but likewise without increase or income; enclosed by 'nothingness' as by a boundary; not something blurry or wasted, not something endlessly extended, but set in a definite space as a definite force, and not a space that might be 'empty' here or there, but rather as a force throughout, as a play of forces and waves of forces[...] do you want a name for this world? A solution for all its riddles? A light for you, too, you best-concealed, strongest, most intrepid, most midnightly men? – This world is the will to power – and nothing besides! And you yourselves are also this will to power – and nothing besides!**

(*The Will to Power*, 1067)

First interpretation: an objective explanation for everything

The traditional view looks to the will to power as an explanation for all of life's manifestations. It is a neutral 'force' that governs the world. The best way to understand this view of the will to power is to look at the quote from the collected notes *The Will to Power*.

This passage has its attractions in its picture of the world as a 'monster of energy' and seems to point to a belief on Nietzsche's part in some underlying principle, a 'theory of everything'.

To support this interpretation, some scholars would cite the importance of the pre-Socratics for Nietzsche who, on the whole, were distinguished by the belief that there is an underlying principle that governs the universe, an archê (first principle) that is the origin of and responsible for all things. For example, the Greek philosopher Thales (c. 625–545 BC) presented a form of **material monism**: that the universe consists ultimately of only one substance. What makes Thales stand out here was to pronounce that there are fundamental features of the universe that are not immediately accessible to the senses or to 'common sense'. It makes us think that the world is not as it at first seems: there are inner workings to be uncovered. Thales was not so concerned with the Homeric gods at play, but adopted a materialist view that all things were made of material substance and it is possible to uncover patterns and laws for this material stuff. Thales, in his case, concluded that the seeming multiplicity of the universe can be reduced to the fundamental substance of water which, of course, is wrong, but at least he began the philosophical enterprise of seeking an underlying explanation for all things.

Is this, then, what Nietzsche's doctrine of the will to power is? A view of the underlying principles of the universe as a multiplicity of drives seeking power over one another? Taken at face value this much-quoted passage certainly seems to assert that the will to power is an all-encompassing phenomenon; the very essence of life itself, '*This world is the will to power – and nothing besides!*' But we need to be very careful of our sources when reading Nietzsche. The above quote is from section 1067 of *The Will to Power* which, as already mentioned, is a work that has been much discredited, as it is really a compilation of Nietzsche's notes edited by his sister who had her own political and ideological agenda. In fact, Nietzsche himself had discarded the passage in 1887, and so he would not have endorsed its publication, thus giving it a printed status it does not deserve.

Those scholars who have attempted to argue that Nietzsche's will to power is a reference to the underlying 'substance' of the world, to the world as a 'monster of energy, without beginning, without end' (*WP*, 1067) have had to rely mostly upon the discredited work *The Will to Power* as their source. Attractive though this concept of the will to power may be, it does not hold up to scrutiny when seen in the light of works that Nietzsche intended to have published. In fact, to suggest that Nietzsche wanted to put forward a 'theory of everything' may well go against what he stood for. For example, when we read what Nietzsche said in *Beyond Good and Evil*:

> *... what formerly happened with the Stoics still happens today, too, as soon as any philosophy begins to believe in itself. It always creates the world in its own image.*

(BGE, 9)

This passage can be read in a number of ways: on the one hand he is accusing the Stoics of imposing a particular view upon nature but, on the other, Nietzsche seems to be suggesting this is something that philosophy *inevitably does*. Whilst he may be criticizing the Stoics for 'creating the world in its own image' he seems to be admitting that this is unavoidable. Therefore, is Nietzsche acknowledging that his speculations on the will to power are an assertion of some underlying fact about nature whilst also being aware that any assertions, any statements of 'facts', are ultimately the philosopher's own prejudices? Such ambiguities are typical of Nietzsche and there is certainly a tension between Nietzsche speaking of nature in terms of universal, natural laws, and his constant warning against engaging in such metaphysical speculation.

Second interpretation: a subjective interpretation

> *... somebody with an opposite intention and mode of interpretation could come along and be able to read from nature, and with reference to the same set of appearances, a tyrannically ruthless and pitiless execution of power*

*claims. This sort of interpreter would show the unequivocal
and unconditional nature of all 'will to power' so vividly
and graphically that almost every word, and even the word
'tyranny', would ultimately seem useless[...] Granted, this is
only an interpretation too – and you will be eager enough to
make this objection? – well then, so much the better.*

(*BGE*, 22)

The final sentence of the quote above is particularly instructive
as it appears to be an admission that his talk of the will to power
is his *own* interpretation and is therefore no 'truer' than that put
forward by any other philosopher. But if it is indeed the case that
the will to power is no more true than any other view of the world,
and if Nietzsche knows he is putting forward his own subjective
view, then why give it any credence? To answer this it is important
to remember how much value needs to be placed on Nietzsche's
style: on his use of metaphor, ambiguity, riddles, humour and irony.
Nietzsche knows he is seeing the world from his own perspective,
for how can he – or anybody else for that matter – do otherwise?
Nonetheless, the knowledge that one cannot demonstrate objective
truths, that one cannot step outside of one's own perspective, is not
a reason to then remain silent or to adopt a nihilistic stance towards
our values. Nietzsche, remember, is very positive; he does not bury
his head in despair and existential nausea (although he has his
moments), but rejoices with the realization that we cannot know
what is true. Nietzsche, however, does not stop using words such as
'truth', 'soul', etc., but these words for Nietzsche mean something
different. He writes about the will to power because *he* values it, not
because it necessarily exists 'out there'.

Given the importance of language and communication for
Nietzsche, it seems appropriate to look to *Thus Spoke Zarathustra*
as it is here where we can find Nietzsche's more systematic
elaboration of the will to power as interpretation. In the
Second Part of *Thus Spoke Zarathustra* – the chapter entitled
'Of Self-Overcoming' – Zarathustra declares: 'Where I found a
living creature, there I found will to power.' The importance of the

title of this chapter in his elaboration of the will to power should not be overlooked: of *self*-overcoming, or *self*-transcendence. Rather than seeing the will to power as some underlying principle of the world, it is seen first and foremost as the power over one's *self*. Reading the story of Zarathustra we have a character in the process of creation: creation of a new kind of world with new values. In this sense, Zarathustra can be seen as mirroring Nietzsche's own philosophical enterprise. When faced with a world that no longer had meaning or credibility in his eyes (and, Nietzsche believed, in the eyes of a select others, though growing in number he thought) he creates a world that does have meaning for him. Again, the issue of whether it is 'true' or not is something of an irrelevancy or, at best, merely highlighting the whole problem of trying to look at the world in polar opposites of 'true' or 'false'. Nietzsche often saw his Supermen as creative artists, painters and musicians and so the importance of creating a world for oneself that has value is a philosophical and artistic enterprise.

Related to this self-overcoming is self-enhancement. Whilst we can possibly survive with a world that lacks meaning, Nietzsche questions whether such a life is worth living. Self-preservation is one thing, but self-enhancement – the bettering of one's self – is another. In fact, mere self-preservation will inevitably lead to decay and destruction, whereas enhancement ensures we survive, and survive as better human beings. The will to power is when we say 'yes' to life and go on the offensive against mediocrity and what Nietzsche saw as decadent values.

What is understood by 'truth', then, is whatever overcomes the world, whatever view of the world prevails. Truth is a mental construct; it is what is psychologically bearable.

Is the subjective understanding of the will to power the most accurate account of this enigma? Whilst a metaphysical understanding of the will to power seems way off the mark given what Nietzsche has to say about metaphysics and those philosophers who subscribe to a world 'out there', we also need to be cautious in arguing that Nietzsche was entirely proposing a subjective, psychological account. His eagerness to devour the writings of his contemporary theorizers in the realms of biology, physiology, embryology and the like, points to a certain degree of empathy for their views. Nietzsche at times can come across as strongly empirical and it would not be too far-fetched to suggest that, although he emphasized the subjective account of the will to power above all else, he ambitiously hoped – perhaps vainly – to underpin it in an empirical account of how the world actually seemed to operate.

6

the Superman, eternal recurrence and perspectivism

In the prologue to *Thus Spoke Zarathustra* (1885), the proclamation is made that the Superman is on his way. The word in German is *Übermensch*, which more literally means 'Overman'. The Superman represents various qualities that we should strive for, such as strength, courage, style, and refinement. The idea of the eternal recurrence seems to be living the same life; every detail again and again. This is not really meant to be an explanation of how the world actually operates, but more of a thought-experiment to determine how you would react if you did have to live this life over and over again. If you can still affirm life then you have passed one of the 'tests' for the Superman. Nietzsche adopted a view of knowledge that is referred to as perspectivsm which, essentially, argues that there is no such thing as absolute knowledge that is independent of our perspective.

Thus Spoke Zarathustra

Thus Spoke Zarathustra, although perhaps not considered one of his most rigorously philosophical works (compared with *Beyond Good and Evil* and *The Genealogy of Morals*) is nonetheless an extremely enjoyable read and can prove very enlightening in trying to understand what Nietzsche has to say about such concepts as the Superman.

Zarathustra is a prophet, an historical figure who possibly existed around 1500 BC and is also known by the name the Greeks gave him, 'Zoroaster'. Zoroastrianism became the official religion of the mighty Persian Empire for around 1000 years, and small groups still exist in Iran and amongst the Parsis in India. The original Zarathustra invented the concept of good and evil as an eternal war of battling opposites. However, Nietzsche's Zarathustra aimed to show that we must go beyond the concepts of good and evil. For Nietzsche, the historical Zarathustra represents what can be achieved through the will to power, and his belief that every person is responsible for his or her own destiny would have rung a chord with Nietzsche.

Thus Spoke Zarathustra is in four parts, the first part being penned in 1883 and the fourth part completed in 1885. When Nietzsche started writing this work he had recently lost his 'family' of Lou Salomé and Paul Rée (see Chapter 2), and he now, more than ever, felt alone in the world. *Zarathustra* is about solitude, and the hero of the book is the loneliest of men. Zarathustra the prophet has returned with a new teaching, having realized the 'error' of his old prophecy. The book is written in a biblical style, with a narrative, characters, events, setting and plot. In these respects it is very different from all of Nietzsche's other works and helps to explain its appeal to a more popular audience.

At first choosing solitude in the mountains, Zarathustra grows weary of his own company and descends to seek companions and to teach his new philosophy. But, even when surrounded by disciples, he retreats once more back into his solitude and praises its virtues. The new teaching that Zarathustra presents is based upon the foundation that God is dead, and, subsequent to this, the teachings on (and striving to become) the Superman, the will to power and the eternal recurrence.

A brief summary of Thus Spoke Zarathustra

The Zarathustra of the Persians was the first prophet to talk of the Day of Judgement, of time reaching a final end. However, Nietzsche's Zarathustra provides a very different teaching:

Part I

'All gods are dead: now we want the Superman to live' – *let this be our last will one day at the great noontide.*

(*TSZ*, Of the Bestowing Virtue)

Zarathustra descends from ten years of solitude in the mountains and expresses the need for a new teaching to replace the old teaching of a belief in God and morality. The new teaching, 'God is dead', will be brought by another teacher: not Zarathustra, but a 'Superman'. However, the masses laugh at Zarathustra and so he sets out to find followers. In this first part it is Zarathustra who perhaps learns more, rather than actually teaches, as he realizes that concepts such as the Superman cannot easily be taught. It is not enough to simply tell the people about the Superman through a series of statements. By the end of Part I he has instead gathered together a small band of disciples rather than attempt to preach to the masses. It is a realization on the part of Zarathustra – and Nietzsche too – that his words are not for Everyman.

Part II

I go new ways, a new speech has come to me; like all creators, I have grown weary of the old tongues. My spirit no longer wants to walk on worn-out soles.

(*TSZ*, The Child and the Mirror)

Having told his disciples to leave him and to find their own way, Zarathustra now looks within himself for enlightenment, returning once more to the mountains. After the passing of years, Zarathustra once again descends amongst his disciples with a 'new speech'. In the section *Of Self-Overcoming*, he talks of the will to power and states that the highest human beings, those who know how to utilize the will to power in the most positive sense, are philosophers. These philosophers, these Supermen, will destroy the values that people have cherished and replace them with new values. They will teach mankind how to love the earth.

Part III

> *'Behold, we know what you teach: that all things recur eternally and we ourselves with them, and that we have already existed an infinite number of times before and all things with us.'*
>
> (*TSZ*, The Convalescent)

This part acts as the climax for the previous two parts. Writing this part, for Nietzsche, was, he reported, the happiest time of his life. For Nietzsche, writing was a form of therapy, but also he believed that reading his works could be therapeutic for the reader. Philosophy as therapy may seem a relatively new idea, but in fact it was something Nietzsche acknowledged too. Zarathustra separates from his disciples and takes a long sea voyage, for he no longer needs disciples. In solitude once more, Zarathustra wills for eternal recurrence, for his 'redemption'.

Part IV

> *If you want to rise high, use your own legs! Do not let yourselves be carried up, do not sit on the backs and heads of strangers!*
>
> (*TSZ*, Of the Higher Man)

Nietzsche had originally intended Part III to be the final. When he wrote a fourth part he only distributed it to around 20 people. It was added in 1892 when Nietzsche had gone insane and was in no position to object to its conclusion. In this part, Zarathustra's solitude is broken by a series of visitors, including a soothsayer, two kings, a scholar, a sorcerer, the last Pope who also believes that God is dead, the 'ugliest man', the beggar and Zarathustra's own shadow! Zarathustra has a 'last supper' with his visitors, preceded by a speech about the Superman. He then engages in question and answer conversation on such issues as the Superman and the death of God.

Many scholars have argued that *Zarathustra* is a better book without the fourth part. However, although the work is certainly more consistent with only the first three parts, the fourth part is very important in terms of understanding Nietzsche's development as a philosopher. Part IV deals with a major concern of Nietzsche: redemption. In *The Birth of Tragedy*, Nietzsche argued that mankind could be redeemed through the revival of Greek tragedy and the renewal of German culture. However, as he became disillusioned with the possibilities of Art to achieve this, Nietzsche still avoided the pessimistic response and believed that there still can be redemption, that there is still a need to revalue all values and overcome decadence. However, Part IV is less naïve as the ironic realization dawns that affirming life can only be achieved by resenting life as it presently is.

The eternal recurrence

A central theme of *Thus Spoke Zarathustra* is the eternal recurrence. In fact, for Zarathustra, embracing the concept was, for him, salvation. What did Nietzsche mean by this? Apart from *Zarathustra*, the doctrine of the eternal recurrence only gets a few mentions in his later works. However, the doctrine was hinted at in *The Gay Science* where Nietzsche presents a 'what if' image. He asks what if a demon were to creep up to you one night when you are all alone and feeling lonely and were to say to you that the life you have lived and continue to live will be the same life you will live again and again for infinity? This life will be *exactly* the same; no additions and no omissions, every pain, every joy, every small and great event. If this were the case, would you cry out in despair over such a prospect, or would you think it to be the most wonderful outlook ever?

Though not mentioned specifically, this 'what if' scenario sums up the eternal recurrence: whatever in fact happens has happened an infinite number of times in the exact same detail and will continue to do so for eternity. You have lived your life an infinite number of times in the past and will do so an infinite number of times in the future. Importantly, like seemingly the doctrine of the will to power, Nietzsche presents the eternal recurrence as a thought experiment, not a provable truth. You do not have to believe the demon is telling the truth, merely to consider the prospect of it being true and the psychological effect this has upon you. Consider the possibility yourself: does it make you happy or fill you with despair? Like the will to power, the aim is to provide an insight into the way we live our lives and, perhaps, even to change the way we live our lives. If indeed we experience despair at the prospect of living this life again and again then it logically follows that we are not happy with the way we live our lives.

Nietzsche considered that merely thinking of the possibility is the greatest of thoughts and would have an impact on how you perceive yourself and how you live the rest of your life. This is why he gave it such central importance in *Zarathustra*. Proof is not important here, only the fact that we may consider it as even a possibility is sufficient. Nietzsche's aim in presenting the eternal recurrence was to present a positive doctrine of an 'afterlife'; one that would not devalue this life.

It is curious that Nietzsche places greater emphasis on this doctrine in his notes and letters than any other aspect of his philosophy, and yet he never elaborated upon it in his published works. When we consider what was important for Nietzsche, what stands out is his belief throughout his life that existence should be *justified*; that is, the true philosopher does not go through life happily in an unquestioning manner, but seeks to give meaning and value to his existence. In *The Birth of Tragedy*, Nietzsche thought life could be justified, could have value, through art, or rather 'Art' in the Ancient Greek sense. The Greeks lived a life of 'Dionysian joy'. However, Nietzsche, later in life, felt that Art was not the salvation he had originally hoped and it was in August 1881, while walking amongst the high mountains in Switzerland, that the thought came to him of the eternal recurrence. With this thought came an experience, a psychological impact that caused him to affirm life and to love it.

This feeling of joy, Nietzsche thought, is the formula for the greatness of the human being, and he is making an essential connection with the doctrine of the Superman. The Superman is one who, like Zarathustra, is able to embrace the doctrine of eternal recurrence and find redemption within it. If, before and after every action, you were to ask: 'Do you want this action to occur again and again for all eternity?' and you could answer in the joyful affirmative then you are exercising the will to power in a positive manner. The weak look to the next life for hope, whereas the strong look to this life.

The Superman

In *Thus Spoke Zarathustra*, the prophet descends from his mountain to teach the Superman. The German word is *Übermensch*, which literally translates as 'Overman'. However, 'Superman' – despite the comic book connotations and the possibility of misleading people into believing in some superhuman figure – remains a common translation. Nietzsche did not invent the term, and would have come across it in the great German poet Goethe (1749–1832) and, in his study as a classical philologist, in the works of the Greek writer

Lucian of Samosata (c. 120–180 AD). However, it was Nietzsche who gave the term a new meaning.

If we consider *The Gay Science*, Nietzsche uses the term '*Übermensch*' to refer to gods and heroes of, especially, the Ancient Greeks. For him, these were symbols of non-conformity, of those who did not fit within the norm but were prepared to challenge contemporary values and beliefs. This is a theme – the stress on individualism and the realization of one's self – that is evident in Nietzsche's earlier works, and a careful reading of these shows the development of his thought previous to the first appearance of the Nietzschean Superman in *Thus Spoke Zarathustra*.

In his *Second Untimely Meditation*, for example, Nietzsche talks about the goal of humanity, and that this must rest with its highest specimens. That is, Nietzsche is aware of what mankind is capable of achieving and raises the question of why we usually fail to live up to our potential. There are examples in history of great people, of philosophers, artists and saints, but even they remain 'human, all too human'.

Nietzsche often sings the praises of Napoleon. Not because of his military prowess but because he represents what Nietzsche calls the 'good European'; the person who is not obsessed with the kind of nationalism that was plaguing Germany at the time of Nietzsche. In this arena, Nietzsche also places such figures as Goethe, Beethoven, Caesar and Michelangelo. However, none of these is a 'Superman', but each represents certain features that make up the will to power, such as self-mastery, individualism and charisma. Nonetheless, in the end all of these figures still remain 'human, all too human', for Nietzsche is quick to recognize their faults. There has never been a Superman, although Nietzsche sees the ideal as a Caesar but with the soul of Christ. Even Zarathustra is only the herald of the Superman, not one himself.

Importantly, the link with the eternal recurrence is that the Superman is one who will embrace the doctrine: who can look to his own life and wish to re-live it again and again for infinity. It is an unconditional acceptance of existence, a saying 'Yes' to everything. For Nietzsche, the Superman is an affirmation of life not, like Schopenhauer, a denial of it and a desire for the self to be extinguished.

On truth and perspectivism

One important field of philosophy is known as **epistemology**, or the theory of knowledge. In fact a number of philosophers would argue that this field is *the* most important task for philosophers to undergo: what can we know with any certainty? The word 'philosopher' is from the Greek 'lover of wisdom' and whilst the term 'wisdom' seems to be rarely used these days to describe knowledge, the primary task of philosophers is the same, and goes right back to the Greeks who asked the questions that still engage us today. How 'wise' can we be? That is, how much can we know and what do we mean when we say we 'know' something to be the case?

For example, someone may feel inclined to make a seemingly innocent remark such as 'the sky is very blue today'. The philosophical response to this would be to raise questions concerning the validity of the statement 'the sky is very blue today'. Is the sky very blue for everybody? When we say it is blue, what colour are we perceiving in our heads? Is the sky itself actually blue or do we only see it as blue? What is meant by very blue as opposed to just blue? How blue can blue be? Would the sky be blue if there was no one around to see it? Can we really know for sure what colour the sky actually is? And so on! In fact, the last question gets to the heart of epistemology. We are unable to step outside of our own bodies. We cannot 'see' the world as it actually is because we see it via our senses. Can we always trust our senses?

Nietzsche's perspectivism

Imagine you are staring at a painting, and that this painting represents the sum of all life and experience. The painting, you might think, is finished. The paint is dry and it hangs upon the wall. For Nietzsche, however, he is not gazing at a finished painting, for it is still evolving and will continue to do so forever. Most people accept 'common sense': that there is a world out there, that when you kick a stone there is an actual stone, that the laws and behaviour so embedded within our lives are so real that they are not questioned. The painting is thick with paint and it is difficult to wipe aside the colours and shapes of earlier generations. For Nietzsche, however, our 'common sense' is merely an *interpretation*. This is Nietzsche's **perspectivism**: we see the world from our own accumulated lives and experiences, but this does not make it *right*. The painting is not an accurate representation of something 'out there', but the imaginings of the human mind.

Common sense, the acceptance that things are how we think they are, is not only seen as necessary for life, but also useful. Nietzsche would not disagree with this. Our 'painting' of the world is not a random collection of colours and shapes, but a purposeful process of understanding the world and adapting to it; that is, our worldview is necessary for our very survival. To this extent, common sense is true in that it allows us to function. This understanding of truth is equated with *utility*: how *useful* is a particular interpretation of the world? By declaring that God is dead, Nietzsche is stating that the belief in God no longer serves a useful purpose.

In *Human, All Too Human*, Nietzsche speculated that there might indeed be a metaphysical world, but at the very best this is just a bare possibility and much too inadequate to look to it for salvation. Here, however, there seems an inconsistency in Nietzsche's thought: is there a real world or isn't there? Truth, for Nietzsche, seems to be equated with workable fictions, yet he also seems to want to say what the world is actually *like*. Here he becomes muddled; on the one hand declaring that the world is a matter of perspective, whilst on the other not entirely denying the possibility that we can have endurable facts. As an example, it is a fact that humans need oxygen to breathe. Are we to say that this is a matter merely of perspective, a truth that we need to survive but that we cannot say that *there really is oxygen, and we really need it*? Are we then presented with a hierarchy of knowledge, some more true than others? Even if Nietzsche were to say, as he seems to, that our understanding of the world all boils down to aspects of the will to power, there is a danger here of introducing his own metaphysics: a force that prevails across the universe.

The importance of language

If we consider the history of thought we become aware that this history is almost entirely full of a belief in gods, a God, an afterlife, and the eternal soul. It is only very recently, representing a small fraction of this timeline, that people have begun to question these concepts. Now, returning to our painting once more: if every brush stroke represents 100 years of the history of mankind, then the questioning of metaphysical concepts amounts to only one such brushstroke, hidden amongst thousands of others. If our worldview is painted in such a way, Nietzsche asserted that so, also, is our language. In *Twilight of the Idols*, Nietzsche famously declared that we would not get rid of God until we get rid of grammar. This view was echoed later by the British philosopher Bertrand Russell (1872–1970) who believed that everyday language embodies the metaphysics of the Stone Age. If we are to establish a better philosophy then we must work out a new language.

Nietzsche argues that the language we speak seduces men. When people use terms such as 'mind' or 'soul' it is so embedded within our language that, as Nietzsche says, we would rather break a bone in our body than break a word. Most of our language is based upon mankind's early use of language, upon a more primitive psychology that we therefore cannot escape from because of our use of everyday language.

Our attachment to our language is so strong we could not readily do without the fictions it describes. Nietzsche also believed that even the language of physics is a fiction, an interpretation to suit us. He talks of the concept of atoms as a useful tool to explain the nature of the universe, but that is all that they are. However, Nietzsche's perspectivism goes much further than this for it is not just theoretical entities such as atoms, but *all entities* that are fictions. All bodies, lines, surfaces, concepts of cause and effect and of motion; these are all just articles of faith but do not in themselves constitute a proof.

There have been philosophers and scientists who have also rejected the world of common sense, but Nietzsche asserts that they then make the mistake of creating another world that they consider to be real. Despite Nietzsche's charity towards science, he does not accept that it has brought us any closer to reality because, for Nietzsche, there is no reality to get close to. Since the time of Galileo in the seventeenth century it has been the practice of scientists to present theories that conflict with the contemporary common-sense view of the world, such as the view that the earth revolves around the sun or that humanity evolved from other species. This has resulted in often radical transformations in our understanding of the world and leads to a new common-sense view. For the scientist, these theories are usually regarded as allowing us to get closer to how the universe really is. For Nietzsche, despite their pragmatic application, they are still nonetheless a fiction. They are no more real than the previous worldview.

Does Nietzsche's perspectivism help to provide us with a clearer understanding of the Superman? Nietzsche's *Übermensch* would not be deluded into believing in a reality that can be attained or comprehended, nor would he look to religion or philosophy for salvation. He would be less concerned with stating what is true than in telling what is false, yet he would also need to be tied to a common-sense perspective if he were to survive; the extreme sceptic would not be able to get out of bed in the mornings.

However, this should not prevent daring experimentation, in seeking a new language and philosophy. Would Nietzsche go so far as to suggest a physical change also? Is he pre-empting the advances in genetic engineering? This, one suspects, would be giving the German philosopher too much credit.

religion
and
politics

It is inaccurate to describe Nietzsche as an atheist, at least in the sense of being entirely irreligious. In fact, Nietzsche, in many respects, was a very spiritual person who appreciated the importance and value of religious belief. It is not important whether religion is true or not, but whether or not it is life-enhancing. There is considerable debate in academic circles over whether Nietzsche really subscribed to any political views. A number of scholars argue that Nietzsche's philosophy is much more of a personal, subjective account. Nonetheless, Nietzsche did write on politics, and he was critical of the democracy of his time. He saw this as 'levelling' and, therefore, discouraging individuals from expressing themselves, although he was not necessarily against democracy as such, provided it allows the Superman to flourish. Nietzsche does not present any one particular kind of political system, but this is not to say he is apolitical.

Nietzsche's religiosity

Nietzsche has often been described in the past as an atheist, and his declaration 'God is dead' would seem to support such a view. Yet an essential appeal of his philosophy is his use of religious language, metaphors and symbols, together with the fact that Nietzsche himself does not escape entirely from his Lutheran upbringing. Further, Nietzsche was specifically addressing an audience at a specific time and place (that is the coming new century in Europe) and what Nietzsche perceived to be an important turning point for Europe: the dawn of a new age in which the old God was dead and society was confronted with an increase in the secularization process. An understanding of Nietzsche's 'religiosity' needs to be seen within the context of his lack of faith in the secular order to provide humanity with any meaningful existence.

Some scholars of the past have certainly acknowledged that Nietzsche has a religiosity. For example, the German philosopher Martin Heidegger (1889–1976) called him, 'that passionate seeker after God and the last German philosopher' and, more recently, the British essayist Erich Heller (1911–90) says of him that, 'He is, by the very texture of his soul and mind, one of the most radically religious natures that the nineteenth century brought forth...'

Nietzsche as a 'sort' of atheist

At the very least, Nietzsche did declare himself a devotee of the Greek god Dionysus. Nietzsche's Lutheran upbringing cannot be totally discarded, for although Nietzsche may not be concerned with the existence or otherwise of God – and does not bother to engage in any of the standard arguments for or against the existence of God – he nonetheless deals with, in the words of the theologian Paul Tillich, what is of 'ultimate concern': how are we to be 'saved'? By 'saved' this need not require the baggage of theological teachings related to salvation, for it is enough to conceive salvation as a concern for the future of the human race *on this earth*. Nietzsche's concern is to replace what he perceived as a pathologically sick belief in a Christian God with a new life-affirming framework for salvation.

An important reason why Nietzsche uses Christian imagery and ideas, even though 'God is dead', is that the death of God does not bring theology to an end, rather to a fresh beginning: the death of God is what makes salvation possible. In *Twilight of the Idols*, Nietzsche remarks, 'We deny God; in denying God we deny accountability: only by doing *that* do we redeem the world.' To do this Nietzsche reaches for Christian imagery.

Nietzsche the Lutheran

A number of factors contribute to Nietzsche's religious outlook: the tight-knit Lutheran background, the influence of his father — a pastor — his piety as a child, the key places of his upbringing all being at the geographical centre of Lutheranism, and enrolment to study theology at the University of Bonn. In fact, Nietzsche saw Luther as one of his heroes up until the time he split with Wagner, and Nietzsche is deeply indebted to Lutheran Pietism, the movement that was prevalent in the time and place of Nietzsche's upbringing. Pietism is essentially anti-rationalist, indifferent to theological speculation and concerned more with instinct; with engaging with Christ on a personal rather than an intellectual level. This emphasis upon instinct is central to Nietzsche's philosophy, as this quote from *The Antichrist* highlights:

> *It is false to the point of absurdity to see in a 'belief' ... the distinguishing characteristic of the Christian: only Christian practice, a life such as he who died on the Cross lived, is Christian... Even today such a life is possible, for certain men even necessary: genuine primitive Christianity will be possible at all times... Not a belief but a doing...*

(AC, 33)

Whilst Nietzsche has been called a nihilist, Nietzsche himself sees Christianity as nihilistic, as life-denying and depraved, in which life can only have meaning by reference to some other-worldly realm. With the death of God, this nihilism is unmasked and Europe is faced with apparent hopelessness, devoid of salvation. At this point – the point at which Nietzsche believed existed in Europe during his time, the post-moral period – Nietzsche sees the opportunity to address the question of whether humanity really needs redemption from the divine: cannot human life be self-affirming? Throughout Nietzsche's philosophy there is a sense of urgency, a recognition that there existed in his time a very brief window of opportunity. He believed that the power of *ressentiment*, of self-hatred (a potent use of the will to power) would quickly regroup under another guise with new prophets. One reason why Nietzsche is so widely read today must be due to the recognition that these new salvations have come under such brands as communism, nationalism, capitalism and other '-isms'.

Salvation, for Nietzsche, is an *internal* transcendence. It is a healing process to cure humanity of what he saw as a disease brought about by attempts to ameliorate suffering through Christian redemption. However, rather than healing, Christianity has made the patient worse. Nietzsche's conception of health is not that of a pain-free state, for he believed pain to be a prerequisite of health. Nietzsche believed that Christianity does not cure, it *anaesthetizes*: it blocks pain and persuades the people that the absence of pain is the same as salvation.

Democracy

Whilst Nietzsche is a great admirer of Athenian culture, the same cannot be said of that other great Athenian invention: democracy. Rather than support the view held by some – that Athenian culture was a result of democracy – Nietzsche praises the flourishing of the arts in Athens *despite* its democracy, and so sees it more of a hindrance to culture rather than a benefactor. In fact, it seems that Nietzsche's dislike for democracy goes back a long way, as he resigned from a student fraternity because he disapproved of what he regarded as a democratic admissions policy.

Already, in his student years, we have a man who displayed elitist tendencies even before he had developed any strong philosophical views.

One point that needs to be borne in mind was that at the time Nietzsche was writing, democracy was something of a 'new idea', despite its origins – though in a rather different form than we know it today – in Ancient Greece. Much of Europe at the time was fundamentally aristocratic, and so the view of democracy would have been very different from what, today, is largely taken for granted and considered by many as the best form of government. Having said that, more egalitarian views were certainly being bandied around during his time, not least from his friend Wagner who argued for the abolition of the state and the introduction of radical egalitarianism. In addition, Meysenbug was also a campaigner for democracy and was exiled because of it.

The crux of Nietzsche's argument against democracy (as well as feminism, socialism and anarchism) is that it is merely a continuation of Christianity: an ethics of equality that weakens the strong and preserves the failures. He believed that in such a political climate, culture would find it difficult to flourish.

It is a mistake to interpret Nietzsche, as some scholars do, as someone unconcerned with society or politics, but rather only centred on the asocial, isolated individual. Nietzsche is deeply committed to the promotion of high culture and sees the role of the individual in an Ancient Greek sense as a citizen, as part of a community. His attack on modernity is an attack on liberal democracy with its features of atomistic individuals lost at sea with no values or meaning. In this sense, Nietzsche is very much a traditionalist.

With the decline in political absolutism sanctioned by divine law, there is the possibility that the state, too, will break apart as political authority loses its reverence. Nietzsche hopes that the increase in the secular will lead to a new period of toleration, pluralism and wisdom if chaos and anarchy are to be avoided. Nietzsche, it should be stressed, is not anti-democratic so long as it leaves space for the rare, the unique, and the noble. Democracy does not necessarily lead to the death of high culture and noble values, provided that culture and politics can give each other space. Nietzsche believes that democracy is the political form of the modern world which is best able to offer the best protection of culture; that is, of art, of religion, of all creativity. In his letters he says he is 'speaking of democracy as something yet to come' and favours a social order which 'keeps open all the paths to the accumulation of moderate wealth through work', while preventing 'the sudden or unearned acquisition of riches.'

Nietzsche wishes to preserve a private/public distinction, whereas modern liberal society – although its ideology of the privatization of politics allows individuals a great degree of private freedom – undermines notions of culture and citizenship. Nietzsche's criticisms are levelled against the prevailing democracy of his time, remembering that most of Europe was still autocratic, but was not against a democracy 'yet to come'. This raises interesting debates, occurring in our current time, as to what forms of democracy are possible and a growing awareness that there is not a one-fits-all political system, as has been demonstrated when attempts have been made to impose Western forms of democracy on non-Western states with devastating consequences. Democratic politics, Nietzsche acknowledges, *can* promote and further culture and, in the recognition that with modernity comes the absence of any possibility of ethical universality, the best hope for the future is that there exists a culture. What kind of culture this would be is uncertain. Would we all agree that Nietzsche's conception of culture, of *high* culture, is one we would accept?

Nietzsche's nihilism is his contempt for what he regards as negative or destructive values, such as democracy, feminism, socialism and other features of the modern world. But it is wrong to accuse Nietzsche of being a nihilist, for a nihilist is only negative and puts nothing forward in its place, whereas Nietzsche is greatly concerned – in fact you could consider it his primary mission throughout much of his life – with a need to present *new* values (even if those new values are a return to ancient values), not simply to get rid of the present ones and put nothing in their place.

On women

Comments on women in *Beyond Good and Evil*

A deep man, on the other hand, deep both in spirit and in desire, deep in a benevolence that is capable of rigour and harshness and easily mistaken for them, can think about women only like an Orient: he has to conceive of woman as a possession, as securable property, as something predetermined for service and completed in it.

(238)

In no other age have men ever treated the weaker sex with such respect as in our own – it is part of our democratic inclinations and basic taste, as is our irreverence for old age. Is it any wonder that this respect is already being abused? They want more; they are learning to make demands; they end by considering that modicum of respect almost irritating, preferring to compete, or even to battle for their rights: let's just say women are becoming shameless.

(239)

Women want to be autonomous: and to that end they have begun to enlighten men about 'women per se' – that is one of the worst signs of progress in Europe's overall uglification.

(232)

Stupidity in the kitchen; women as cooks; the frightful thoughtlessness that goes into providing nourishment for families and heads of households! Women don't understand what food means – and yet they want to be cooks! If women were sentient beings they would in their thousands of years of cooking experience have discovered the most important physiological facts and taken over the healing art!

(234)

Why, if Nietzsche is actually traditionalist, elitist, aristocratic, anti-egalitarian and sexist, does he appeal so much to modern liberal, free-thinking men *and* women? Whilst part of this appeal may well be due to Nietzsche's unique and modern style, his clever use of metaphor, irony, ambiguity, and so on, it is certainly inadequate to be satisfied with this and simply ignore the actual *content*. Nietzsche, for his part, was out to criticize *European* feminism particularly, in the same way that he attacked just about everything in Europe during his time: nothing escaped his scatter-gun. Feminism was just one of those features of modernity, with its origins in the French Revolution and its ideas of equality. Nietzsche could, and indeed *has*, been conscripted into the feminist cause to some extent by some feminist scholars by emphasizing Nietzsche's attack on equality as an enemy of the Noble spirit: the aristocratic figure, or the philosopher-king if you like. Seen in one context, the Noble spirit can encompass women as well as men in that it is essentially an attack on nineteenth-century egalitarianism that diminishes self-worth rather than women *as such*. However, these may be seen as a somewhat generous reading of Nietzsche.

The philosophers of the future

In *Beyond Good and Evil* especially, Nietzsche talks of the philosophers of the future, Nietzsche's comments on these leaders – especially given the German word '*Führer*' – has resulted in many misunderstandings, with visions of blonde Aryan beasts oppressing the masses. It still begs the question, nonetheless, who these philosophers of the future would be and what exactly would they do? Those who would argue against any political agenda at all would see these philosophers as essentially free-thinkers, artists, musicians and so on, whereas Nietzsche's use of such terms in *Beyond Good and Evil* as 'commanders and lawgivers' (*BGE*, 211) seems more akin to Plato's philosopher-kings legislating over a new form of society:

> *I am talking about an increase in the Russian threat so great that Europe would have to decide to become equally threatening, that is, to make use of a new ruling caste in order to gain a will, a terrible, long-lived will of its own that could set itself goals over millennia...*

(*BGE*, 208)

Nietzsche's philosopher of the future is not just a codifier of values, but a *creator* of values, a lawgiver, a legislator, and this is why Nietzsche sees such figures of history as Napoleon as a philosopher more than he does, say, Kant. Like Plato's philosopher-kings, Nietzsche's philosophers will be compelled into action, although the temptation to retreat into solitude through disgust with society will be great. In many respects the new philosopher will be like Zarathustra, compelled to go down and encourage people to act. He will be the bad conscience of his age – disagreeing with the majority opinions – and will be derided as such. These new philosophers will also be experimenters, not dogmatic in their views.

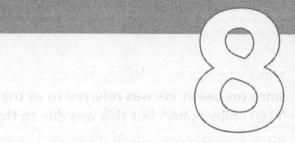

Nietzsche's
legacy

Nietzsche has been hugely influential since his death. He was referred to as the 'Nazi philosopher', but this was due to the propagandist methods of his sister Elisabeth. Nietzsche himself would have been horrified to be associated with Nazism. On the continent, his influence in philosophy has most notably been connected with France and existentialism, particularly amongst such important figures as John-Paul Sartre and Albert Camus. Outside of philosophy, he has impacted upon such literary figures as George Bernard Shaw, and Thomas Mann, and Hermann Hesse. The psychologist Sigmund Freud (1856–1939) apparently thought highly of Nietzsche, as did Carl Jung (1875–1961). The Austrian psychologist Alfred Adler (1870–1937) founded a school of 'individual psychology' where the emphasis on power dynamics is rooted in the philosophy of Nietzsche. The American novelist, philosopher and playwright Ayn Rand (1905–82) was likewise inspired by the writings of Nietzsche.

It has been said that Nietzsche was in no way a racist, except perhaps towards his own nation, the Germans. More accurately, he hated what Germany had become; a nation of people who were nationalists, rather than 'good Europeans' and, worse, who were discriminatory towards others. It is a sad irony, therefore, that he became the official German philosopher. During World War I, Elisabeth Nietzsche proclaimed her brother as an imperialist and a warrior who would have been proud of the Germans' cause. She arranged for copies of _Thus Spoke Zarathustra_ to be sent to the troops.

However, it was with the arrival of the dictators that she was really able to promote Nietzsche's philosophy. She heard that the Italian fascist dictator Mussolini had claimed that Nietzsche was a great influence on his politics, and so she made a point of establishing a regular correspondence with him. Mussolini took the notion of the Superman to mean anyone who stands out from the crowd and controls his own destiny. In fact, he saw himself as one of these Supermen, and Elisabeth praised him as the new Caesar.

When Elisabeth chose to stage a play written by Mussolini at the Archive, the Italian leader was unable to attend. However, the leader of the National Socialist Party, Adolph Hitler, was present that night. This was her first introduction and she immediately fell under his spell. It was at the Bayreuth Festival on the 50th anniversary of Wagner's death that Elisabeth Nietzsche and Adolph Hitler discussed Nietzsche's philosophy. Nietzsche later became the official philosopher, giving Nazism the intellectual credibility it otherwise lacked.

Needless to say, after World War II, serious academic study of Nietzsche was neglected as few wished to be associated with the 'Nazi philosopher', yet Nietzsche's own comments on Germans and the German nation may well have resulted in imprisonment or worse during the period of Nazi Germany if they had ever been allowed to be aired in public. Aside from his sister's active encouragement, what other reasons could there be for associating Nietzsche with Hitler?

1 One reason is Nietzsche's association with the Wagners. Richard Wagner himself was an anti-Semite and the Wagners as a whole have been associated with National Socialism. As a consequence any disciple of Wagner is an implied disciple of National Socialism, despite Nietzsche distancing himself from their influence in the late 1870s. As an example, one of the leading figures and theoretical inspirations for Nazi thought was actually an Englishman, Houston Stewart Chamberlain (1855–1927) who became a zealous Germanophile and, significantly, wed Richard Wagner's youngest daughter, Eva. Chamberlain wrote an extensive anti-Semitic text called *Foundations of the Nineteenth Century* (1899) which, though a rare thing to find these days, was a bestseller during the rise of Hitler, alongside *Thus Spoke Zarathustra*, and so already these two books were being linked in the German mind.

2 Another reason is that Nietzsche's caustic writing style bears strong similarities to Hitler's, especially in the last two years of Nietzsche's sane life when he became much more rhetorical, combative and violent in tone. This kind of hatred and venom, though usually in Nietzsche's case an attack on Christians, is not dissimilar from the language used by Hitler to attack the Jews. In *Mein Kampf* (My Struggle), for example, Hitler used terms such as 'parasite' and 'spiritual pestilence'. However, whereas Nietzsche's solution to the problem of prevalent Jewish and Christian values was largely peaceful in tone, focusing on a revaluation of values, Hitler's solution was, alas, far more extreme. Nonetheless, the concern for both was essentially the same in that both strived for a healthy culture and looked to certain sections of humanity that were considered unhealthy. It was in their methods and focus that they differed drastically.

3 Another possible reason for Nietzsche's association with National Socialism is that although he was anti-German in many of his remarks, he was a strong believer in community,

in the *Volk*. Nietzsche contrasts this form of German romanticism with the seeming emptiness and plurality of modernism; in the poet Hölderlin's (who Nietzsche read voraciously) words, the 'destitution' of modernity. Nietzsche shared the romantic's criticism of modernity, with its emphasis on Enlightenment reason, and stressed instead the importance of community and the role of religion within it (see Chapter 8), but what he distanced himself from was the romantic association with nationalism. *Volkish* thinking became indelibly linked with German nationalism and figures such as Heinrich Riehl (1823–97), Paul de Lagarde (1827–91) and, importantly, Richard Wagner. Coupled with this German nationalism was anti-Semitism. Despite Nietzsche's own remarks he was inevitably associated with these figures.

Twentieth-century French philosophy

It could reasonably be argued that to understand twentieth-century French philosophy you have to understand Nietzsche. Nietzsche, travelling from one country to another for much of his life, was a true European, and it was French culture especially that he had a soft spot for, despite the fact he spent little time there. Of course, he likewise often spoke admiringly of Muslim countries and culture, yet never spent any time *at all* in a Muslim country.

For its part, France was slow to take on Nietzsche in the philosophy departments, but when it did, it did so by storm. In fact, it was not so much the philosophy departments that took up Nietzsche to begin with, but the country's writers and artists. One such writer, although something of a philosopher, was Georges Bataille (1897–1962). Under the influence of Nietzsche's views on the Apollonian-Dionysian dichotomy.

Jean-Paul Sartre (1905–80)

This view of the world as essentially a result of waste products, of a world of dead bodies, flies, dirt, mucus, urine, pus, muggings, phlegm, vomit, dandruff, etc. was the reality portrayed by the existentialist philosopher and writer Jean-Paul Sartre. This world is difficult to face unless we comfort ourselves by creating ideals; illusions in which to cope with the mundane and horrific. The experience of 'nausea' which is described in his novel *Nausea*, is actually a form of enlightenment, an awareness of what it means to be alive. In *Nausea*, the character of Roquentin encounters the world of people and inanimate objects and sees things as having the stamp of his existence upon them. This gives existence a nauseating quality, and 'nausea' is an expression also used by Nietzsche in works such as *Thus Spoke Zarathustra* and *Beyond Good and Evil*. Coupled with this concept of nausea is the realization that attempts to deal with objects, situations and people in a rational matter is absurd, and this led to a whole school of Absurd literature.

Albert Camus (1913–60)

In the case of the Algerian-born French author, philosopher and journalist Albert Camus, for life to be meaningful we must live every moment like a person who has just come out of prison and smells the fresh air, feels the sunlight and the ground below. This life-affirming attitude is akin to Nietzsche, and Camus considered his thoughts to be a reaction against nihilism. Whilst Camus tried to disassociate himself from any philosophical schools, he was, as a result of his own writings, inevitably linked with existentialism and the Absurd. While Camus never provides a specific doctrine of the Absurd, he nonetheless writes of experiencing the Absurd in, for example, the novel *The Stranger* and in his essay 'The Myth of Sisyphus'. In this essay, Camus highlights the absurdity of existence by demonstrating that we live a life of paradox: on the one hand valuing our own lives and striving to make something of them, while on the other hand being aware that we are all mortal and so our endeavours will ultimately come to nothing. Camus' aim was not to depress everybody, but rather to consider how we face such absurdity. In fact, he didn't think that life was meaningless: meaning can be created by our own decisions and perspectives, even if this is a temporary thing. This focus on no universals and the death of God – and therefore the death of any kind of absolutes – again was the concern of Nietzsche who likewise rejected nihilism as an option. Camus' philosophical novel, *The Fall*, considers the will to power in the context of the weak who, as a final resort, gain a sense of being better than others because they admit they are ridden with guilt.

Henri Bergson (1859–1941)

The Two Sources of Morality and Religion (1932) is the French philosopher Bergson's only published work which mentions Nietzsche by name, but Bergson's philosophy is Nietzschean in many respects. Like Nietzsche, Bergson sets out to reverse Platonism by presenting what has been referred to as process philosophy. That is to say, philosophy does not unravel permanent truths – which would be Platonism – but rather truth is a process involving time, perception, change, memory and intuition. Like Nietzsche's critique of modernity, Bergson attacked mechanistic philosophy of his time, arguing for intelligence as evolutionary and adaptable. Interestingly, Bergson's philosophy had a major influence on the Greek novelist Nikos Kazantzakis (1885–1957) who also read Nietzsche and produced a version of process theology, expressed in his major work *Zorba the Greek*. According to Kazantzakis, when we look at the source of religion we see that God is the product of whatever people value.

Thomas Altizer (1927–)

The influence of Nietzsche on theology is also evident in the writings of Thomas Altizer who helped to create a death of God theology which may strike some as something of an oxymoron, but was nonetheless an attempt to address Nietzsche's concern that Christianity of the time was leading to nihilism. By God's 'death', Altizer is actually referring to the crucifixion of Jesus Christ which, he says, resulted in the pouring out of God's spirit into the world. God's spirit, then, is not transcendent any more, but immanent: it exists in the material world, in the here and now.

Gilles Deleuze (1925–95)

Like Nietzsche, Deleuze sets out to understand the moral actions and beliefs of people as deriving from their desires and quest for power. To live well is to fully express one's power; that is, to go to the limits of your own potential rather than look for transcendent, universal standards to live by. In *Essays Critical and Clinical*, Deleuze outlines what we must do in the face of a world that is one of flux and difference: 'Herein, perhaps, lies the secret: to bring into existence and not to judge. If it is so disgusting to judge, it is not because everything is of equal value, but on the contrary because what has value can be made or distinguished only by defying judgement. What expert judgement, in art, could ever bear on the work to come?'

Michel Foucault (1926–84)

Perhaps no other French philosopher is more closely associated with Nietzsche than Foucault. Like Nietzsche, he interpreted the world in terms of the will to power and, again, like Nietzsche, had a genealogical agenda which he referred to as 'archaeology': an experimental method which he employed to study aspects of modernity. In the same way an archaeologist literally digs to put together how a society lived, Foucault 'digs' at the form and content of language used in fields of knowledge to reveal the hidden interests of those engaged in discourse, that is, in the dissemination of knowledge. For example, as he states in his work *Discipline and Punish*, when experts (lawyers, psychologists, parole officers and so on) judge on a person's criminality, Foucault sees this as an exercise of power over the criminal. In actual fact, Foucault argues, there is no objective valuation of what a criminal is, and what counts as criminal behaviour in one culture and at one time, can be regarded as legal in another. Like Nietzsche, Foucault attacked Enlightenment attitudes to such concepts as inalienable rights, for Foucault would argue that there is no such thing as a universal good. Whilst arguing for no absolutes, Foucault would not allow himself to be drawn into an ethical system or a political agenda. Foucault saw it as his mission to *investigate*, not to advocate.

The analytic tradition

The **analytic** movement dominated philosophy in Britain and the United States for most of the second half of the twentieth century. Like existentialism, it is difficult to identify specific tenets of this movement, although most analytic philosophers argue that the primary aim of philosophy is, or should be, to look to how language is used. Language, it is argued, is the basis for all our knowledge and so when we use concepts, the important thing is to consider how those concepts are used in the context of language.

It is interesting that whereas existentialism tends to emphasize the irrational and emotional side, the analytic tradition is much more rationalist and logical. Yet Nietzsche succeeds in straddling both traditions. Although Nietzsche is not such a direct influence upon the analytic tradition, much of his philosophy is considered to be firmly within this tradition, particularly his criticism of past philosophers for preoccupying themselves with metaphysical questions and also his view that it is not a matter of 'true' or 'false' but whether a claim makes sense that is important. Further, Nietzsche understood the importance of language in defining our world.

One branch of the analytic movement is called **logical positivism**, which adopted a criterion of meaning which stated that unless a statement can be verified by experience (for example, 'all bachelors are happy') or is true by definition (for example, 'a bachelor is an unmarried man') then it is meaningless. This inevitably results in metaphysical statements being discarded as irrelevant to philosophy because such statements like 'God is wise' cannot be proven by experience and nor is it by definition the case that 'God' and 'wisdom' are synonymous (although some have argued that in fact they *are* synonymous).

Art

In literature, Kazantzakis has already been mentioned, as has the fiction of Sartre and Camus. Other writers who have been influenced by Nietzsche and, in fact, have written on Nietzsche, include Thomas Mann (1875–1955), Hermann Hesse (1877–1962), and George Bernard Shaw (1856–1950).

* In the case of Mann, he was particularly interested in Nietzsche's views on the connection between sickness and creativity, which comes across especially in his novel *The Magic Mountain*. Like Nietzsche, Mann argued that disease should not be seen in a wholly negative way, because life and great creativity can come out of illness.
* Hesse's novel *Steppenwolf*, especially, portrays the Nietzschean loner, the 'beast', or 'genius' in the character of Harry Haller who feels out of place in the world of 'everybody'. Hesse lived in Basel for a time, partly because he saw it as the town of Nietzsche.
* Shaw's play *Man and Superman* comes directly from Nietzsche's ideas on the Superman.

Other famous writers influenced by Nietzsche include André Malraux (1901–76), André Gide (1869–1951) and Knut Hamsun (1859–1952), whilst Nietzschean themes crop up amongst the beat poets such as Allen Ginsberg (1926–97) and Gary Snyder (b.1930). Mention should also be made of the Jewish American painter Mark Rothko (1903–70) who was influenced especially by *The Birth of Tragedy*. Rothko saw the mission of art to address the need for modern man to be redeemed from the horrors of life through myth. Rothko regarded himself as a mythmaker as is evident from the titles of so many of his paintings: 'Antigone', 'Oedipus', 'The Sacrifice of Iphigenia', 'The Furies', 'Altar of Orpheus' and so on.

Other influences

The list, quite frankly, is virtually endless. In Russia, the **Symbolists** – who proclaimed art to be the new religion and the Superman to be the artist – adopted Nietzsche's philosophy. Nietzsche's future-orientated philosophy, of man as a bridge to a higher man, influenced revolutionary thinkers such as Trotsky. The psychologist Sigmund Freud (1856–1939) thought highly of Nietzsche, as did Carl Jung (1875–1961). The Austrian psychologist

Alfred Adler (1870–1937) founded a school of 'individual psychology' where the emphasis on power dynamics is rooted in the philosophy of Nietzsche. American novelist, philosopher and playwright Ayn Rand (1905–82) was likewise inspired by the writings of Nietzsche.

Nietzsche, no doubt, will continue to influence new generations on a variety of different levels, whether due to his artistic style, the fact that a reader can pick on one profound sentence and write a novel around it, or due to his philosophy specifically which has outlived the man and his age and is as applicable to today's society as it was to Nietzsche's time and the horrors that engulfed Europe in the twentieth century.

Glossary

Amor fati means to 'love your fate' – a term Nietzsche used to express an affirmation of life.

Analytic the tradition in philosophy that emphasizes the importance of language in our understanding of the world.

Aphorism a concise, pithy and often clever saying, varying in length from a single sentence to a short essay of several pages, expressing a general truth.

Correspondence theory of truth the view that when we talk of things being 'true', then we are referring to things that actually exist in reality. When you point to an object and say 'it is there', then it *really is* there.

Darwinism a reference to the theories propounded by Charles Darwin (1809–82). Darwin is the founder of modern evolutionary theory.

Dualism the philosophical position that there are two worlds: the physical and the non-physical.

Empiricism the philosophical position that we can acquire knowledge of the world through direct experience of the senses.

Existentialism the philosophical movement that emphasizes human freedom.

Idealism stresses the importance of the mind in understanding what we can know about the world. At the most extreme, it argues that there is only the mind, no external world.

Logical positivism an expression of the analytic tradition in philosophy; it argues that statements are meaningless if they cannot be verified.

Metaphysics the speculation on what exists beyond the physical world, such as the existence of God, what is real, and so on.

Modernity a term with many meanings, but generally a reference to the increase in secularization accompanied by a belief in scientific progress.

Monism the view that ultimately reality is composed of only one substance. It is, therefore, opposed to dualism.

Nihilism literally a 'belief in nothing' although there are varying levels of nihilism. At the less extreme it is a rejection of contemporary values and traditions, but does present the possibility of alternatives.

Noumena metaphysical beliefs about the soul, the cosmos and God, which are matters of faith rather than of scientific knowledge.

Orientalist a term used to describe Western writings and writers who present a romantic and distorted picture of the east, or the 'Orient'.

Pantheism the belief that there are not two worlds, but one and this is identified with God.

Perspectivism the view that we perceive the world according to our perspective, although this may not be as the world actually is.

Phenomena in Kantian terms, the world of everyday things that we can detect with our senses.

Philology the study of language and literature.

Pragmatic theory of truth the opposite of the 'correspondence theory of truth'. Something is only 'true' to the extent that it is practical to believe in it.

Rationalism the philosophical position that reason, the intellect, forms the basis for much of our knowledge.

Relativism morals and beliefs are a product of a particular time and place and, therefore, there is no such thing as 'right' and 'wrong'.

Ressentiment the French word for resentment. Nietzsche uses it to explain his genealogy of morals. *Ressentiment* is the hostility that the slave feels towards the master.

Timeline of important events in Nietzsche's life

1844   Friedrich Wilhelm Nietzsche born on 15 October in Röcken, a small village near Lützen.

1849   Death of Nietzsche's father on 30 July, diagnosed as softening of the brain.

1850   Nietzsche's brother, Ludwig Joseph, dies on 9 January. The family relocates to Naumburg in early April.

1856   Nietzsche writes his first philosophical essay, 'On the Origin of Evil'.

1858   In October he is accepted into the Pforta School.

1862   Together with a few friends, he founds the literary club 'Germania'.

1864   In October he begins studying theological and classical philology in Bonn.

1865   Leaves Bonn and moves to Leipzig to study philology. He has given up on theology. In October he discovers Schopenhauer.

1868   Becomes friends with Wagner.

1869   Appointed to the University of Basel.

1870   Military service as a medic. He falls ill with dysentery and diphtheria.

1872   *The Birth of Tragedy* is published. It is rejected by scholars.

1876   Becomes friends with Rée and attends the first Bayreuth Festival. He makes his mind up to break with Wagner.

1879   Resigns from university teaching and starts his nomadic life.

1881   His first visit to Sils-Maria. Has his great 'inspiration' and writes of eternal recurrence.

1882   Proposes marriage to Lou Salomé twice.

1883   Death of Wagner on 13 February.

1885   Nietzsche's sister marries Bernhard Förster in May.

1889	Nietzsche breaks down and never recovers from mental illness.	
1900	Dies on 25 August.	

Chronology of major works

Birth of Tragedy (BT)	**1871**
Untimely Meditations (UM) **1**	**1873**
2, 3	**1874**
4	**1876**
Human, All Too Human (HAH)	**1878**
The Wanderer and His Shadow	**1880**
Dawn (WSD)	**1881**
The Gay Science (GS)	**1882**
Thus Spoke Zarathustra (TSZ)	**1883–85**
Beyond Good and Evil (BGE)	**1886**
The Genealogy of Morals (GM)	**1887**
The Twilight of the Idols (TI)	**1889**
The Antichrist (AC)	**1889**
Ecce Homo (EH)	**1889**
Nietzsche contra Wagner (NW)	**1889**